THE COLOR OF LIGHT
Poems for the Mexica and Orisha Energies

Odilia Galván Rodríguez

ACKNOWLEDGMENTS

With special thanks to Awo Ifajembola, Francisco X. Alarcón, Jane Norling, Edward Vidaurre, Sharon Elliott, and Aquene Aquetzalli for their kind input.

Some of these poems have appeared in the following publications: Poetry of Resistance: Voices for Social Justice, University of Arizona Press, 2016; Our Spirit, Our Reality: Celebrating Our Stories, Wheatmark, 2011; Migratory Birds: New and Noted Poems; ZYZZYVA; La Bloga; Poets Responding (a Facebook Page) Dedicated to Poetry, Poetics, and Social Justice; Love and Prayers for Fukushima and the World - WordPress Blog.

Copyright © 2019 Odilia Galván Rodríguez

All rights reserved under International and Pan-American Copyright Conventions. Published in the United States of America First Edition.

Cover information: Cover art copyright © 2017 Keena Romano. "Oracle Visions," water color and paint pens on paper.

Cover / book design © 2019 Carlos Galvan.

All inquiries and permissions requests should be addressed to the Publisher.

Library of Congress Cataloging-in-Publication
Galván Rodríguez, Odilia
THE COLOR OF LIGHT
Poems for the México and Orisha Energies
Odilia Galván Rodríguez—1st ed.
p. cm.

ISBN:0692183507
ISBN-13: 978-0-692-18350-2

1.2.3.

Dedication

To all the protectors of Earth and

In loving memory of my father Gilberto Rodríguez Paredes and mother Antonia Galván Longoria, who now reside in The Color of Light.

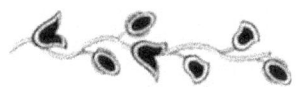

Contents

Introduction i

The Energies ~ Esu-Elegua and Tezcatlipoca 1

She Walks in Beauty 4
Border Inquest Blues 5
Dancing for Life 7
Destinies 8
Yellow Face (Ixcozauhqui) 9
More Dark Dreams 11
Undercurrents 12
Pulchritude 13
The Web of Life 15

The Energies ~ Ogun and Xipe Totec 17

Xipe Totec 20
Poem 6 – Night Train 21
Civilization's Drugs 22
Salvation 24
The Blues From Reds 25
The Greening 26
On the morning commute – 2011 28
Circling ~ 29
Flying Away 30
Sweet Teeth 33
Xoxoctli – 35

The Energies ~ Ochoosi and Camaxtli 36

Cloudy Serpent 38
Of Wars 39
Transmitting Peace 40
Tribeswoman's Cicatrices 41
Poem 15 ~ Mazatl (or other names for Horses) 42
Camaxtli 43
Purple My Heart 44
News Clips 47

Tule Fog Dreams 48
Night Wings 50

The Energies ~ The Obatala and Quetzalcoatl 51

The Loosening 54
Going North for Winter 55
Sinuous Soliloquies 56
Convergence 57
Dimensions 59
Survival 60
Quetzalcoatl 62
Patents on Life 65
Most Precious Twin 68
Morning Star 69

The Energies ~ Oshun and Xochiquetzal 70

For Protection 73
Cantes a Palo Seco (a cappella) 74
Rearranging 76
The Distance of Love 77
Gitana's Prayer 78
Parallel Universes 79
Ololodi 80
In the Pact of Closed Mouths 81

The Energies ~ Oya and Tlazolteotl 85

Invocation for Tlazolteotl 88
Ofrenda (Dos) 89
On the Veranda 91
Wounds 92
Deep Breathing 93
Yansan 9 94
Cuando Muere La Tarde ~ When Afternoon Dies 95
Body Oracle 97
Copper Hands 98
Days of the Dead 101

The Energies ~ Yemaya and Chalchiuhtlicue …. 102

Diosa …. 105
Bella Luna …. 108
Five Senryū …. 111
In Between Sleep and the Light …. 112
Chalchihuitlicue's Story …. 114
Mother of the Fishes …. 115
La Llorona's Sacred Waters …. 116
Intervention of Angels …. 118
Of Sepia Toned Mysteries …. 119
Water Song …. 121

The Energies ~ Shango and Huitzilopochtli …. 122

Dreaming Huitzilopochtli …. 125
Chocolate …. 126
Kolonial Legacy …. 127
Blue Hummingbird On The Left …. 128
Six in the Mix …. 129
The Blues for Saxophone …. 130
Transformations …. 131
Prickly Pear Hearts …. 132
It's No Sin …. 135
Insomnia …. 136

The Energies ~ Orunmila and Tlaloc …. 138

Rainmaking …. 141
Ofrendas …. 142
Poem 30 - Earth First …. 143
Teocintli …. 144
The Color of Light …. 145
In the Line of Time …. 147
La Vista …. 148
Poem 3 ~ Destiny …. 150
A Blessing of Blue Corn …. 152
Oracle …. 153

About the Author …. 154
Bibliography and Sources …. 155

Introduction

What this book is and is not. This is a collection of poetry dedicated to some of the principal energies of the Mexica and Orishas – two nature-based spiritual/cultural traditions, and ways of life. The Mexica indigenous energies are still quite alive and well in Mexico, and in the diaspora – due principally, in my humble opinion, to the Danza tradition. I have felt akin to these energies since I learned of their existence, on a road trip to the states of Guanajuato, Jalisco, Morelos, Michoacán, and Puebla Mexico, when I was a teen. I'd never been to Mexico before and when invited by my best friend and her parents to accompany them on a family visit for a month one summer, I jumped at the chance. These energies were everywhere, depicted in all kinds of indigenous art, in architecture, in weavings, in clothing, in the vast wares available in the markets, in museums etc. I went around asking lots of questions to learn a bit about their importance and history from talking to people and reading. The Orishas, representatives of Olodumare, the Supreme-Creator-God, I've known about since I was a little girl. Having grown up in public housing on the south-east side of Chicago which housed people from just about every culture, some of my Cuban and Puerto Rican friends family's talked about Orishas. And from what little I could glean from asking my curious but respectful questions, I learned that they were different from the Catholic Saints, that we all had in our homes and which often represented them but were as important. I'd later learn about the forced synchronistic nature of both of these traditions due to colonization and all that brought with it to the diaspora.

Ifa-Orisha is an ancient spiritual tradition which comes with and from the West African Yoruba peoples. They practice this living breathing way of life, which spread throughout the diaspora mainly because of the forced migration of the Yoruba peoples brought to the Americas and forced into slave labor. Today, the tradition has spread to practically all parts of the world because of the migrations of Ifa-Orisha practitioners, many of them Cubans. As a woman in my late 30's, I became very close to the Orishas and was helped quite a bit by initiates of this tradition during a period of great upheaval in my life. Of all the spiritual traditions I have studied and practiced, Ifa continues to figure prominently in my life.

In addition to political science, which I majored in during my university studies as an undergraduate, I have always been drawn to comparative religious studies. Particularly to spiritual traditions practiced by peoples for thousands of years before the "New World" conquests. The imposition of Christianity, under the guise of civilizing "the savages," is what the colonizers brought along as part of their arsenal of death and oppression. It was part of their genocide, which included the erasure of the peoples cultural and spiritual traditions. Cutting people off from their spirituality, languages, music, dance, art, and ancestors was their plan for total domination and/or decimation. I was raised Roman Catholic and while I always felt the rituals of the church were beautiful and powerful, especially when mass was still held in Latin, the tradition never really felt as though it wholly belonged to or embraced me and mine.

Later, I would find out that my father was actually descended from Conversos – Sephardic Jews from Spain, who during the Inquisition were forced to renounce Judaism and convert to Catholicism or die. This would explain a lot of why he would only attend church twice a year, if that, my father too had the legacy of erasure in his DNA not only in the blood passed down from indigenous ancestors.

I give thanks, to all of the Indigenous peoples of Mexico and the various traditions of Danzantes who to this day venerate the Mexica energies by observing the traditional Mexica calendar and hold celebrations in accordance with it, and to the people of Cuba who practice La Regla de Ocha, and similarly in Brazil, the people of the Candomble tradition of Orisha worship which was conserved for many years in secret by the ancestors brought from Africa. It is our great fortune, that despite violent attempts to wipe them all out, they were able to keep these nature-based spiritual/religious traditions alive. This says a lot, not only about the strength of character of those who survived and passed down the teachings, but also about the power of the traditions themselves, that continue to this day.

In the first incarnation of this book I was calling the energies "deities" and later came to realize after talking with practitioners and elders that this label could be confusing because the Orisha and the Mexica energies are not seen as gods or goddesses in the eyes of the people or those whose traditions these energies belong to. Moreover, these energies play an important role in communicating with the natural world and to the greatest energy – the One who created us. Even though the definition of deity also includes denoting the divine nature of God, and these energies like ourselves, are certainly manifestations of the Creatrix, nevertheless, I agree that it is misleading to use the word deity to describe them.

The energies function as conduits, divine messengers, helpers, and wisdom keepers. In both of these spiritual traditions, there is but one supreme Creatrix-God. Please note that the descriptions of the energies contained in this book are not all inclusive nor are they meant to be exhaustive of the vast and rich historical and/or liturgical teachings and wisdom available to practitioners and people who live these ways. The information provided herein is basic, for those who have little or no knowledge of these tradition's existence or survival. They are also provided for those who may have knowledge about one of the traditions but not the other. If you see any parallels between them you may wish to learn more.

For all the ancestors who had the tremendous ability and dedication to honor, preserve, and pass down these rich and beautiful traditions - I give thanks. Asè O! and Mexica Tiahui!

Song to Esu Odara

Èsù, Èsù Òdàrà, Èsù, lanlu ogirioko. Okunrin orí ita, a jo langa langa lalu.
Divine Messenger, Divine Messenger of Transformation, Divine Messenger speaks with power. Man of the crossroads, dance to the drum.

~ Oriki Esu Odara
(Praising the Divine Messenger of Transformation)

Con Flores Escribes

Con flores escribes,
Dador de vida
con cantos das color
con cantos sombreas,
a los que han de vivir
en la tierra.

With Flowers You Write

With flowers You write,
O Giver of Life
With songs You
give color,
with songs You
provide shade
to those who will
live on the earth.

~ Nezhualcoyotl, King of Texcoco (1431-72)

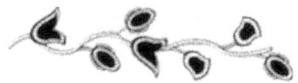

The Energies ~ Esu-Elegua and Tezcatlipoca

Esu-Elegua the Orisha, or energy who opens and closes all doors of positive possibility on our life's path. He is considered the quintessential communicator who as divine messenger, is armed with the knowledge of all earthly and heavenly languages and is bestowed with ability to facilitate communication between human beings and the divine. Esu as a force of nature is primarily associated with the crossroads – be it the meeting of two country roads, two paths crossing in a forest, or at an intersection in any of our planet's urban areas. Esu's energy, along with that of his other warrior brethren, is especially powerful in the woods. One of his most important roles is that of divine enforcer of justice, and because of this, people sometimes characterize him as being devious or cruel. In his energy we learn the concept of divine balance and choice. We all have choices and must live with their consequences.

Like the trickster-magician in most nature based traditional cultures, Esu reminds us of who we are. He holds humanity to the divine rules of the universe and of nature. He reminds us that we are all humble creatures, a part of the greater web of life. And, as all the creation has equal status, Esu acts as the great equalizer. We are all related and must interrelate. His justice can come in the form of a small slap on the wrist, or something that feels akin to a twist of fate. Esu's shifting of situations are opportunities to learn life lessons, to see situations in a different light, and yes, to laugh at ourselves.

Esu resides in the betwixt place, between Orun, the other realm, and earth. He serves as one of Olodumare's (God's) chief messengers and is honored at the beginning of all ceremonies as he is the one who carries the word, of all offerings and ebos [sacrifices] made by earth people, back to Orun. Without Esu's participation and approval nothing can move forward.

In the Regla de Ocha of Cuba, Esu, along with the other warriors Ogun and Ochoosi, protect the Ile, or home-temple, against danger from outside forces. In different Yoruba spiritual traditions his colors are red and black, white and black, or red. The numbers 3, 11, and 21 represent him.

Tezcatlipoca is also known by the names of, Mirror that Smokes, The Shadow, He Who is at the Shoulder, One Death, Yellow Face, The Enemy on Both Sides, and Smoking Mirror, among others. His name may also have been taken from the word Tezcapoctli or shining smoke, the people's word for soot which contains shining metal flakes, and which is used to paint Tezcatilipoca's image. It is also the name given to the black obsidian mirrors used by medicine people. Tezcatlipoca has a major role in the Danzante tradition and is historically one of the most revered and well-known energies of Mexico. He is an old energy and is said to have been venerated by the Toltecs and later adopted by the Mexica. It is said that he embodies the darker or shadow aspects of Quetzalcoatl. His energy is not only called upon by warriors but is also evoked when calling the energy of the earth and the universe itself. He represents the study of psychology and the validity of introspection.

A canto in the Florentine Codex to Tezcatlipoca seems to relate that he, like Esu- Elegbara of the Yoruba, was viewed as the purveyor of justice in life. That he is an energy prayed to for blessings and that it is he who opens or closes the doors on the path of destiny. This revered energy was also honored on all road and street crossings with a stone seat known as Momoztli, which was decorated with flowers replaced every five days. Tezcatlipoca is also said to be a trickster, revered particularly by soldiers and magicians.

Tezcatlipoca is said to have the gift of invisibility; he is an energy of the night represented by the color black. He can be identified in the codices by his hair, which is often depicted as cut in two different layers, a characteristic of warriors, and by a mirror drawn in the place of one of his feet that was torn off by the earth monster. Tied to his right foot is a deer hoof which represents his speed and agility. His nahual is the jaguar.

To Esu-Elegua and Tezcatlipoca in gratitude for smoke and mirrors, and sacred directions.

She Walks In Beauty

she walks
in beauty
in night
shadow dreams
a star specked shawl
swirled across
her shoulders
free of wide world's weight
tonight she dreams
reality that fits
she strolls
red earth mesas
where gold bones
are a sunken treasure
all that is left
of petrified trees
rock roots
in an ancient ocean
transformed
to desert floor
deep with messages
of the still rooted

Border Inquest Blues

at what crossing
could my poems
become bread
or water
to offer a people
the thousands
who cross so many miles
of misery

perched on trains
like birds
with clipped wings
who only fly
in their dreams
but decide to search out
the promise
of a better life at any cost

which of my
careful word choices
make a difference
to scorched tongues
that can no longer
even form a whisper
let alone cry out for help
in a desolate desert

there are no
flights
on 747's
for a people

with only prayers
without papers
thick with words
that legitimize them
in an illegal world
full of legalized criminals
who form tempests
to tease out fear and who
year after year
think up new ways
to hate
at the same time take
even a person's last breath
if it benefits their profits

at what checkpoint
do my words become more
than arrows sharp in their bite
or mere criticisms
of the "Right" that
do not hit the target
of putting an end
to this war

Dancing for Life

cool wind at sunrise
loosed the light fog
from dark claws
undressed the day

dance-dream visions
chokecherry flesh
blossoms thick
the tree of life

humble offerings
our prayer-ties
twisted tight
flown multicolored

day undressed
sun merciless
on the altar
of our flesh

Destinies

a bag
of seeds, of songs.
Kokopelli trickster
plays on his flute in a desert
canyon

doom words
still full of hope,
want to spill out on parched
ground. desires water to live ~
more life

with this
drumbeat. I give
you back your heart, my heart.
let's dance back the clouds and rain ~ our
duty

a rock
can hurt or heal
like you – who dash through time,
as though there are no tomorrows ~
to live

beneath
trees we made love,
and more than fruit was born.
a future we could not foretell ~
our fate

Yellow Face – Ixcozauhqui

he who looked for light
spent his life searching
for brilliance
but was marked
to live life
as the guardian of night
with its sorcerers and
covert creatures
who preyed
on the lonely and
the sick
the fearful
the most dis-eased
of mind
but in his dreams
he lay in fields
of golden corn
of sunflowers
and heady marigolds
the yellow corn pollen
showering down on him
with butterfly wing softness
in slow motion

the golden eye overhead
forever vigilant and
shining down on him
on the land
on his desire
to live in the daylight
soon these rays of light
his dreams of brightness and of day

even in the darkness
became his waking obsession
he shone with desire
to change his life and
one sleepless night he spied
a piece of flaming star-
seed that sparked hot
it fell from the sky
a sliver of brilliant light
which he captured
and turned to molten flame
in the palm of his hand

Yellow Face
got his name
when he discovered fire
which he tended and
never let go out
he was Firekeeper
no longer only of Night
now graced with this gift
he could light up
the azabache sky and make all the
slithering things scurry
into deepest shadows

now the people called him
Ixcozauhqui
and when he looked
into the jet mirror of the lake
his silver-speckled
piñon pitch reflection
his never before seen face
glowed golden
in the firelight

More Dark Dreams

mas sueños
clouds of black birds
burst and rush
toward flames
fire's wind roars
go silent
then we hear
husks unbury
after lying
four years dead
in leaves
they flower
these new cicadas
who call out
for a mate
not there

dark water weeps
can loss be so
severe
cicadas fall
silent
crows perch
wooden and tall
trees explode
white-lightning
moon's face
hidden
in their story

Undercurrents

another black box silence
voices disappeared
like so many others
mysteries and tangled webs
but just after midnight
tiny obsidian butterflies
swing in to tell the story
in fluttering wings
their whispers fall
on sleeping ears
receivers wake flustered
know they've forgotten
something

get an all day
just on the edge
of something itch
a nagging feeling
a tip of the tongue
remembrance
which spawns restlessness
at night they lie wide-awake
dream of old telegrams
in Morse code and
Spirit voice
that won't be quieted

✿ Pulchritude

translucent
the cobalt night
poppy's orange
caught in river's
obsidian reflection
stars rushing
sonorously over
ancestor's bones
those rocks
smoothed over
by their song

while in cities
barren horizons
of urban misery
a people tattooed
with the scourge
of daily life
the hate of the haves
for the have nots

no   beauty
in constant
asphalt
though humans
adaptable
to surroundings
find the occasional
grandeur

those rogue flowers
deviant in color
but stronger
burst forth
in garbage heaps
or up through shimmering
summer sidewalks

neo-code talkers
read the codices
dispute tales of
the Rapture's empty
end-of-the-world
scenarios
our world has and
will continue
to transmute
we will seize
the fake tabloid tidbits and
people's fear of loss
will be masticated and
spit out as seeds
of new hope

The Web of Life

broken
our pieces are
puzzles to put us back
together. while weathering storm's –
darkness

to heal
we need spirit
light, enlightening us.
how can we believe in nothing –
and live

to live,
not just exist,
to feel all, real and raw
all our truths that have left us skinned –
jangled

we self-
medicate to
eradicate effects
of what's been left. in beauty – we
all rise

out of
what should have been,
annihilation sure.
our hearts still beat on the earth –
sprouted

tendrils,
firm roots that reached
our ancestor's power,
from there we were newly born - our
children

time is
not a line, it's
a circle-web of life
that can never be undone – by
hatred

The Energies ~ Ogun and Xipe Totec

Ogun in the Lucumi African spiritual tradition is described as a warrior Orisha who lives deep in the forest; he is an expert hunter and ironworker. He is credited with forging civilization, because without metal objects our modern cities would not have been built, nor our means of mass-transportation: the trains, planes, vehicles, roadways, bridges etc. He is also known as the energy who deals with obstacles in our life's path, with his machete he cuts them down. While Esu-Elegua opens our roads and doors, it is Ogun who goes in as point person to make sure that everything is all clear. He is the patron of metal workers or those who use metal tools in their trades, from the butcher to the surgeon. He protects all warriors, and all those whose work requires them to use knives, machetes, swords, axes, or guns, etc. They all can use Ogun's blessings to be safe.

There is a part of Ogun's spirit energy which deals with survival through necessary assertive or even aggressive action. This can manifest in our lives to clear away obstacles that are stunting our spiritual, emotional, or material growth. Ogun is an energy of intelligence, he tempers force with other forms of conduct attributed to a good warrior such as vigilance, patience, and knowing when to act. Compared to the working of iron, the heating and cooling of iron ore, Ogun's energy can also be expressed as expansive and contracting as in knowing when to strike and when it is best to retreat.

The part of the body that belongs to Ogun is the feet, where the force of the ancestors enters the body. He is evoked to guard against accidents, especially against vehicular ones, and for protection against street violence. He is represented by metal objects, particularly the mighty trains, his colors are green and black, and in Candomble – dark blue. His number is 4, and in some traditions his day of veneration is Tuesday however, in the Lucumi traditional Ile he is propitiated on Monday's alongside the other warriors, Esu and Ochoosi.

Xipe Totec "Our Lord the Flayed One," is also venerated as Tlatlauhqui Tezcatlipoca, "Red Smoking Mirror," or the red Tezcatlipoca. He is considered the energy of springtime, of renewal, planting, and of reinventing oneself. As the energy of renewal, and new growth, Xipe Totec rules over the east, the region of light and therefore fertility, and life.

He is legend to have been a pockmarked savior who tore out his own eyes and flayed himself in atonement to God, who in turn gave corn to the people and saved them from starvation. He, having given up his own skin for humankind, was then clad in robes of gold. It is said that he would afflict those who did not venerate him properly, with boils, blisters, and festering sores. Represented in codices as a red Tezcatlipoca with all of his clothes and adornments depicted in this color and his face painted red with yellow stripes. His nahual, or spirit animal, is the Eagle. Xipe Totec, also the patron of gold and silver smiths is revered throughout Mexico and Central America.

To Ogun and Xipe Totec in gratitude for learning how to find discernment in all things, the wisdom of knowing when to retreat, and that in suffering the shadows of hard lessons we oftentimes find the light.

Xipe Totec

i was born red daughter
of the flayed skin
i wear all their skins
their speech skins
clothes skin s
job skins
car and
house skins

i can speak like them
think and act like them

inside
i am as earth
i survive
beneath the new
green blanket
of springtime

i wear skins
wear skins to survive
skins that come complete
with fiery tongue

Poem 6 – Night Train

she hears the train coming
before she sees it
lightning sparks up track
there are lots of passengers
some are never coming back
this train's taking them
forward into time and space
as they race to their destiny

a destiny that should be painless
as morning being birthed
from a natural death
when night loosens its embrace
and day falls from its grip

she's divined her future
read all the signs
in shiny fallen leaves
in crows cawing
in goose flesh and shivers
in the space between raindrops
even in a stranger's eyes that she past
while running in the shadows
under the 99 freeway

she knows
as first light peeks
through the curtains
she's been given another day
to wish upon all she hears
in those throaty whistles
of all the trains that call her name

Civilization's Drugs

Then, shiny glass beads
dangled in their fish belly fingers
as their mouths cicada-called
steady and so bright like
their colored cloth
and hammered iron pots
that while strung up
next to our meager white shells
looked all new and gleamy
or so many of us thought
until the white sugar and
flour commodities
followed by whiskey
poured down
some ancestor's throats

now, plastic money
shiny fast cars
the latest designer clothes
GMO and fast food
computers and flat screen TV's
blinking loud with all their
shiny lies called news
all part of the latest
prescription drugs
to numb our senses
to keep a people defenseless
and mindlessly entertained

while our lives traded like pelts
the land raped and stripped

reminiscent of our warrior's
cut to the quick
just another notch
on some cavalry soldier's belt

our children bent and stooped
in fields carved out
by cruel and shiny knives
that cleared our ancient trees
whose roots talked
and told the crops to grow
to cover up the crime of all time

sown in the peoples blood
that flowed in rivers
across burnt land
fertilizing bitter
the fruit
poisoned by greed
but heeding the call to survive
our people ate and
still strangers try
to force feed US
their lies and trinkets

Salvation

all those iron ponies
with their sleek metal flesh
transporting civilization
and their things in iron bellies
revved-up chests, diesel and oil pumped
power sucked from mother earth's depths
now they too are just another dying breed
like the dinosaurs; and humans
have pushed whole species and
entire peoples off the buffalo jump
their languages, cultures, ancestral homes and
who cares or mourns their death?

most human beings
only know to use and horde
then dump the mess
man-made material things
all expendable
we are such a small part
of the whole of creation
most of us don't remember
our original instructions

we've forgotten
to use only what we need
to use our imaginations
our dreams to change
the road we're on
before it is too late
for our salvation

The Blues From Reds

steel mill blue collar backbones
made for strong shoulders
for our future to stand on

steel city urban jungle
that flowered our kind
we continued to climb

skyward like blue stars
we became two of a larger flame
while all singing the name game

we'd watch the vats of slag
that steamed fiery red along the tracks
of our Steel City blues neighborhood

they foretold a life for us
one that can emerge from the melded down
like shiny steel, our will to thrive stayed strong

The Greening

ancestors greening
the gray mixed light
rain plays a symphony
on train station's tin roof

creation a continuation
of our stars charted
for survival
reveals itself

en una mezcla
su Egungun
Indios y Africanos
reborn in wise eyes

they rise in the red-browns
of the Americas
Ogun breathes
his sweet-green breath
into new possibilities

blesses this mess
of cultural collisions
while we endure
living with the enemy
within and all around us

there is a new circling
of the wagons
challenging us
to create or destroy
we question hate
know their knives

always sharp and
at the ready

while we question
the moon looms bright
now there are but few omens
codes pointing to new roads

ancestors left us
the knowledge
of how to survive
the planned extinctions

we've the distinction
of inheriting codices
bloodied and scorched
still powerful
though presumed dead

burned down to ashes
in pyres built to expire
the people and then hide
horrors of their genocide

but the glyphs rise
our children's wide eyes
reveal possibilities
of lessening our casualties
in future cataclysms

we've been here before these wars
when pyramids hummed deep in
jade green jungles
where people peered out
behind Ek Balam eyes

On the morning commute - 2011

I am not afraid
I can see in the dark
a brilliant flame illuminates me
every morning on my way to work
I say my prayers on the BART train
it could be any God who listens
from here in this train's belly

eyes closed I bow low in my seat
to a God few people riding know
not the one of things
but of spirit
of pure rhythm
the sound of wheel on track
of sincerity
of miracle of breath
pushing in and out
of words formed
on tongue and lips
said in belief and
not just in case
there is really someone up there

I open to the brilliance
but in the background hear
fearful voices, people whispering
someone call security, someone must come see
about that man bent over – there; they think, he may
have a bomb or a gun… might be singing his death song
might be a determined suicide, on the morning commute

Circling ~

two   wild   red-tail hawks   circling   each other higher and

higher faster   faster dangerously surfing winds like waves

until crashing   we fall   we're free   falling

we said so-long   but were spared   seventh heaven's mouth

wind is   funny that way we stand in ripe tulip trees   the

color of shell   say some vows   then get lost on star's   twinkle

what Spring

does   for young hearts   hawks mate for life so what's the worry

flowers   throw off their blouses   their fragrance   deafening

        tiger-

lilies peek their green heads out from the dead red earth   while

puppies   sleep standing   we peel   in smoky stages

              listen to songs

still too green   Spring does that   sometimes calls for crashing

courting   singing   and the only dangerof newness

is its growing old   as soon as it's born

Flying Away

for Gavilan

early morning
calla lilies open happily
as the bottle brush sway
camellias curtsey
the geraniums still slumber
deep purple and
blood-red bougainvillea drape
over terracotta bricks like
a spring waterfall
singing into blue clay pots
shaped like round quiet faces
staring into the sun

monarchs fly south
all this way and
I hope they caught
a glimpse of you
a few weeks ago
in Santa Cruz
before leaving and
that a bold one
flutter-kissed you
on your round
succulent cheek
I so miss kissing you
seventeen years is a long
cut out of a rock
like me

here I sit

in a beautiful *jardín*
of a house carved
into mountainside
it overlooks
a busy riverbank
at night from way up here
I can see all the twinkle star-

lights of Mexico City
and Popocatepetl
just erupted again
it's old but still smoky
like those chipotle chiles
I missed so much

I imagine you
so many miles away
stepping out
of your childhood skin
but keeping it close
instead of tossing it
trying on adulthood
like a new tuxedo
you look in the mirror
but you're not too sure
it's you or if you could
ever really see yourself in it
though the new feel
is tempting
anyway

I'm here (starting)
another life without you and

though my right arm
has not really been lopped off
(still) there's something
essential missing
the pen keeps gliding
across the page and
my muses salute the sun
while perched comfortably
in the fig and plum trees
alongside escaped parrots
who show off their tail feathers
and wolf-whistle at me
while the yellow canaries
(that flew all the way here
from an elder's patio in Morelia
who purposely left their cage door open –
so on the very day

her soul would leave her body
she could fly with them
as she passed on into eternity)
sing sweetly

like the canaries
I too sing
a new-day sun song
sit here and think of you
and remember the future

Sweet Teeth

i

it was another coming
a truth telling
no more clenched teeth
lips holding in the night
we move naked
out into the light

ii

thorns in hearts
the past aching to be set free
reminds us that ignoring lessons
is just more self-sabotage
and while arms twisted can bloom
fields of wildflowers why not sing
your sorrow to the mother of the sea
in hopes of never having to sad-sing again

iii

unearthed
a wedding basket full of blue corn seeds
in wind etched terra cotta pots filled fresh
with water from the great green saguaro plant
sand paintings in coral turquoise and jet
tell of an ancient past
tomorrow's blueprints buried deep
in a kiva dark   a yesterday mouth

iv

euphoria
wraps them as they enter at first light
seeking the iridescent yellow in fields of green
in season the tender rain tears slip into the earth
quenching snakes that bless the corn helps it grow tall
after the harvest we sit under the stalks eat the sweet teeth
it is our gold our body our blood a call to home
planted in the deep blessed earth we are never alone

Xoxoctli –

for JRL

verde como nosotros
when we met
in that long ago yoliztli
cuando éramos verde
green como el maíz tierno
like our love we thought
would last siempre
but forever is a long time
y los verdecitos no saben nada
del tiempo ni como se mueve
más rápido the older people get
pero un yollotli nunca olvida
el teteyollocuicatl of their lover
a heart that flowers

xoxoctli
in yuh (así como) tu y yo
cuando creíamos que éramos todo
lo necesario to live a life in love y juntos
always lo vivimos así hasta que no
you went your path y yo lo mío
but always you had a temactli ipan no
(poder sobre mi) and I was only safe
when I didn't know where tu corazón latía
couldn't feel it calling me from so far away
now I hear it dondequiera que voy
lo oigo y me persigue me llama tú corazón

Nahuatl words – xoxoctli: green. yoliztli: life. yolotli: heart. in yuh: like. teteyollocuicatl: heartbeat. temactli ipan no: power over me

The Energies ~ Ochoosi and Camaxtli

Ochoosi as he is known in the Lucumi Yoruba spiritual tradition of Cuba, is also known as Ossosi, or Oxossi, in Africa and Brazil respectively. He is the embodiment of the master hunter and tracker who shares the forest with Ogun. He is a master shapeshifter, and you never know the path he will take. He is a traveler, in dreams and in time. Ochoosi hunts down our problems and rains down his arrows on the opposition to the progress in our lives. His spirit force is also associated with the ability to leave one's physical body in order to travel the astral plane or to shape shift.

There is much mystery associated with Ochoosi as a sorcerer; he is a master at blending in and becoming invisible. In Cuba, he is associated with jails and prisons and is invoked by people who are having problems with the legal system, or authorities of any kind.

He is venerated along with Ogun. His main attributes are the bow and arrow, and antlers. His colors are violet, green, brown, and gold. Some of his offerings include smoked fish, yams, and mangoes; his main condiment is epo, red palm oil.

Camaxtli, also known as Lord of the Chase, and Mixcoatl, is venerated by the Mexica along with other ancestral and warrior divinities. The Mexica believe Mixcoatl to be Quetzalcoatl's father who was represented in legend by the great Milky Way. Camaxtli is pure Deer Energy a legendary hunter/warrior hero of Chichimec origin. Annually he was offered a great feast by hunters, as he is attributed as a great hunter who discovered many innovations in the art and skills of hunting.

Camaxtli's image, where it existed was made of wood, carved into the form of a man with long hair, his forehead painted black. His arms are adorned with silver bracelets with arrows inserted into a knot at the center of them, in his right hand he held a basket, and in his left, his bow and arrows. At the feet of the icon was a jar, which contained the tools to make fire, along precious feathers which all represent the hunt.

To Ochoosi and Camaxtli for the mysteries of the forest, of shapeshifting, time travel, and of the hunt.

Cloudy Serpent

down
from the milky
sky road
ripe
we were
thrown
in handfuls
from on high
seeding the earth
from molten
blue stars
we became flesh
from your
downy plumes
you made
flores bloom
as humans

Of Wars

There are all kinds
little ones
we fight every day
the traffic
growing old
our souls
moving over
things we fight to change
though we feel we cannot
like the bigger injustices
corporate wars
racism
that murders
and poverty
the silent killer
that lives under
bridges
in cardboard boxes and
other makeshift houses
of homeless people
in barrios
on reservations
the U.S' most shameful ghettos
on countless streets
of a heartless world
that turns away
the growing fray
of people
who cannot pay

Transmitting Peace

hear my
language, it's more
than sign. it's not code for
what rises, within me a fresh
river

we know
all life's sacred
from budding to its death,
and rest in the knowledge of our
elders

I am
more than the red
river that flows through me.
flesh bone fat electricity
fire

you, me,
if all of us
just had a love supreme—
what a different world we'd be,
shining

wired
for ancient sound—
I transmit messages
of love, hope, and tranquility.
for peace

Tribeswoman's Cicatrices

between what is
seen and unseen
in a spirit's heart seek

that hunts new rhythms
for one's closest
woman heart

sometimes our soul
echoes the cries of our whole tribe
we mourn our losses and all that's been stolen

as unfrozen streams try to stem
their own flow we measure our anger
because we know the dangers

as women born with codes
we seek and track justice
to thrive we dream answers

as women who birth new ideas
we seek and find more love
      for the world

Poem 15 ~ Mazatl (or other names for Horses)

Sacred

dogs, holy deer.

our people laid down red

cloth, for you to walk across, oh

Horses

Camaxtli

Lord of the Chase
we paint our faces
lapis lazuli
vision you in your place
alongside all the greatest
warriors from before Rosa
and Emma, Sojourner y Celia
before Crazy Horse and Geronimo
Fidel y El Che
you have no use
for the meaningless

while alive
you tracked down evil
those who run amongst the deer
cannot be seen clearly
you sat in the highest branches
at the height of sky
long enough to sight your prey
on the run to meet the afternoon
where it dies once more
night eyes brilliant and shining
on the path of ocelotl
picking up the pace
the chase just as important
as the capture

Purple My Heart

Para mi 'apá

purple my heart
at nine years old
watching the man, I loved more
than anyone in the world
sitting in the blue-red light
coming through
the picture windows
holding in his strong hands
the case that held
all he had to show
for all those hundreds
of lives he'd taken

their spirits brought him
countless sleepless nights
or took him in and out
of the other side
with night sweats
the wake-up screaming
nightmares
full of those violet faces
of his ghost sickness

purple the heart
my father won in Korea
then his trophy case
shattered and split
with dried seeds of his blood
on still clenched fist
all his medals torn apart
ripped and wrinkled ribbons

resting on splintered glass
meaningless medallions
tossed aside in disgust
him repeating over and over
I did this for what?

purple the oath
of loyalty
my father took
pledged his life
to defend his country
from the Reds
but after all was said
the speeches of good will
could not quell the visions
of those who looked up at him
from charred fields of death
where his big guns had buried them
mirrored back were the faces of kin
they claimed him more
than the white man did
when he returned
home from Korea
jobs and housing
barred to him
and his kind

purple the smoke
of burning cedar and sage
of lavender oil rubbed deep
into head. chest hands and feet
elders predicted
there was not enough
their medicine could do
no amount of ceremony

could wash away
that much blood

the sickness
would have to fade
like the signs of fire
flood or earthquake
with the years
he'd have to pray
away the madness
await his destiny

purple the sorrow cloth
lining his coffin and
covering the mirrors
after his death
rain through
street lamp glow
the sunset
ripple clouds
in a sky so blue
amaranth amethyst
heliotrope lavender
lilacs lupines crocuses
new flowers
on a hero's grave

purple the night's light
seeping through
my window
his candles
on the dresser
lighting the dark

News Clips

when Humpty-Dumpty
finally has his great fall
the peoples defense
against the tech-no-logic empire
will go unpunished
we who reflect
the natural world
shall have overcome
emerging victorious
from the cave
of our insistence
that this myriad
of mixed messages
in the name of
mass communication
the right to know
transparency
our human rights and freedom
from forked tongue speech
a mere echo
of our unanswered screams and
the system's psychobabble
designed to keep us
numbed and confused
we shall wave no new flags or dogs
forever more
there will be no more false freedom of choice
to buy their version of happiness
our message will not be social media-ized
but rather cheered in the forests the parks
in town squares up and down mountains
from sea to shining sea

Tule Fog Dreams

for ML

you walk out into a hazy dream
Tule fog thick but nothing sticks to you,
nothing stops your determined walk of kings,
warriors, or gunslingers that lead
with their left foot stepping sure
always – ever onward to victory –

that's you in this dream
you are in your late twenties
longish raven hair, wavy but not unruly
your features sharp and commanding
as if you are better than everyone else
but later I find out that is not you,
not who you really are, just
how you appear to others –
less sure of themselves.

you are a young man but not a kid
you've already seen plenty of action
in your years on the planet and don't
plan on taking any shit from anyone.
yet, you have those eyes that let out
a bright kindness in the way they shine
especially for the very young, the elderly,
and for the women you love.

you walk out of a haze into a dream
at first you don't recognize me
(I don't recognize me)
talking to a group of men you tower over
and continue eyeing me

standing on the edge of the scene
looking out of place, there are only men present,
I am new to this here that stands in the middle

of nowhere wrapped in swirling fog
almost thick as cotton
yet, my line of vision to you unobscured
it's as though you SEE into me,
every minute of me - since I first
began to tick, since the first spark of breath
that leapt my spirit into flesh and
that recognition scares and shakes me
because even I don't know me – yet.

it is fall and the wind is cruel
turns up the soil that swirls up
off the fields and mingles with the rain
comes down in dirty sheets
the roads become muddy soup.
by then, we are behind locked doors
your hands search my body
trace every line ever written
you whisper incantations
sealing me into you forever and I,
knowing *forever* is only then, let you.

this is how never forgetting someone starts
how it penetrates bone and heart
how we get tied-up-tight to people
who we've always known
been bound to
made pacts with in other lives
in whispers, in sighs, in dreams
in love making, and invoking
Tule fog on rainy nights.

Night Wings

her night wings itch
evening came and went
now swimming in deep sea night
which is finally cooling down
she salutes the blood moon smiling
in the lapis lazuli sky while readying
her lungs to take flight

sometimes she rises from the ocean
like a feathered serpent, or ocean water
that has separated from the soup and
married the wind to become hurricane
pero esta noche se unirá a *los tlatemoani*,
and come sizzling down from the sky
swinging from lightning, or not

maybe she will just take a leisurely flight
around the city to see what trouble she can find or
maybe get some other poor souls out of
she likes doing that sometimes

cooler air has buoyed up what is left of the heat
now there is a real chance of some clean rain
that metallic and baked earth smell is ratcheting up
she stops to wonder where you've been hiding all this time
then unfolds her wings, and flies out into the unknown

The Energies ~ The Obatala and Quetzalcoatl

Obatala is also known as Orishanla, Orisala, Ogiyan, and Oxala in the Candomble tradition of Brazil and is sometimes dubbed the principal deity of the Yoruba. He embodies the characteristics of peace, harmony, purity, clarity, calmness, and wisdom.

In most of the religious-spiritual traditions, which descend from the Yoruba culture, Obatala is considered to be the father of the vast majority of the Orishas and as he controls the head, is considered to be the father of all human beings. As creator of humankind, Olodumare assigned him to help bring humans into the world, and it in one story it is said, that Obatala decided to shape them out of clay.

Obatala has several caminos or paths, one in which he manifests as a very wise and elderly energy, another a warrior, one as a female, as well as others. Some consider him to be an androgynous energy who embodies both male and female attributes.

Principally invoked by those desiring children, prosperity, the curing of illness and deformities, for health, peace, and harmony, Obatala is also asked to help us in matters of bone health, principally our pelvis and spinal column. He is the Orisha of purity, and is represented by white cloth, snails, elephants, and the number 8. Many of Obatala's initiate's prohibitions include the use of any substances which alters consciousness, as this interferes with the clear headedness of the individual which is of major importance in Obatala's integrity.

Quetzalcoatl is also worshiped as *Ehecatl*, Energy of the Wind, and known by many other praise names throughout Mexico such as, Most Precious Twin, Precious Feathered Serpent, Plumed Serpent, and Morning Star; and in the Mayan regions as *Kukulcan/Q'uq'umatz*. He is considered to be the energy which embodies self-sacrifice.

Quetzalcoatl a principal energy of the Mexica, is legend to have risked going to the land of the dead along with his twin brother Xolotl to steal the bones of humans who had perished in a previous apocalypse. He was successful and brought humans back to life by using drops of his own sacred blood in order to resurrect the race. In another story Quetzalcoatl turned himself into an ant and returned to the land of the dead to bring back corn seeds to feed the new humans. As a result, we are considered to be his children, and he is also attributed with having discovered agriculture.

Lord of Healing and magical herbs, he is attributed with being a symbol of wisdom and learning, and of the arts. It has been said that nine different Toltec kings, also named Quetzalcoatl, succeeded the original incarnation of Quetzalcoatl. He is always depicted as benevolent, who shared with and taught the peoples science, the calendar, and devised ceremonies. It is also said that Quetzalcoatl did not want to be propitiated or honored with *chalchihuatl* (sacred blood).

In the codices, Quetzalcoatl is depicted wearing what is called a Wind Jewel, an amulet made from a conch shell. His head is adorned with a jaguar bonnet or sometimes with a small cap, from which a sharp bone protrudes. From here it is said that the blood which nourishes his nahual, the quetzal bird, flows. He is often portrayed with a beard to represent age or depict him as an old man. At times, he is depicted wearing a red mask covering his mouth in the form of a bird's beak, which is believed to identify him as the energy of the wind. He is considered the divine being of civilization, the arts, metallurgy, fate, and of the wind in all its forms including the life-breath.

To Obatala and Quetzalcoatl in gratitude for the wisdom of using our heads and learning to always strive to walk in a good way.

The Loosening

her hair

white as moonlight. loosed.

backlit. a frosty glow.

she brightens the world

with her words. freed.

Going North for Winter

winds scoured the earth
rains followed their fierce footfalls
floods drenched deep drank towns

ancestors sent signs
rounding out nature's warnings
with storytellers

oracles in bones
shells rocks and seeds
read in them our life stories

worth living fully
free from the fear of losing
not bullied by want

leaves are turning birds
flying south for winter
we Heyokas go north

Sinuous Soliloquies

a force
of nature, her mind
dissected in pieces.
rich ruby fruit ~ electrified
fences

..
pennies
on her eyelids
copper helps her sleep deep
dreams, of old stills in the forest ~
lost youth

...
by wind
undisturbed sounds
swimming ceaselessly, calm
on the dead air, lilting a wing ~
pinging

....
a tap
on crystal glass.
syncopated sirens
contact from the past. trilling tongues ~
evolved

―――
woman's
taboo, to wield
thick bullroarer's rope whirled
in hopes of calling a spirit ~
long gone

Convergence

conjunct
my moon and your
Venus rising, like a
prizefighter who refuses to
stay down

I'm all
for harmonic
convergence if it stops
wars for greedy corporations'
pockets

rockets
to the moon left
an indelible mark
on rabbit's left cheek, she seeks peace
daily

land on
a deal, to save
the earth from extinction.
it's really a no-brainer if
we stop

check our
tech-no-logic
brains at the door, open
our hearts, we really want love to
triumph

hippies
were heart people,
who got inspired by
an indigenous worldview. flew
freak flags

higher
than kites kiss skies,
a new way of thinking
backwards, which led forward into
new ways

to think.
reject those life-
ways that are about greed.
about superiority
over.

things change.
some people loved
money and things more – than
themselves or humanity, went
backwards

it's not
all lost. my stars
still shoot, and I wish on
my father's eyes, twinkling brightly
over

Dimensions

blues air

new dimension

pretentious portents

pickled in prophecies

centuries older

than the coldest glaciers

and if all truths contain lies

what flies in the air

falls short of its line

in the sands of time

Survival

to survive grassroot
alliances one learns
to trust likely
suspects turned allies
those who must possess
and continually express
in word and action
tenacity of conviction
for what is just

..
Olmecs lived long
before antediluvian
shadows cast down more
darkness
on an enlightened world
the lightning rods and rain
of their Indo-African gods
brought a new epoch
to the uprooted
and seemingly
washed away

...
it is purely academic
to discuss marsupial beings
without understanding
indivisible bonds
between mothers
and children
no matter their age
distance in geography
or current relationship

....
our species spins
we shed our skins
redefine selves again
and again in a world
that confuses popularity
and material possessions
with sacredness

―――

Pulque Keeper ever vigilant
for it is the plant people
who piece together
the broken and slashed
those who survive
despite great odds and
are made whole again

―――
　.

for survival
sadly we must pass on
to our children
those hard lessons learned
teach them the gift of invisibility
to shapeshift into the acceptable
especially in these most dangerous times

Quetzalcóatl

el Kukulcan anda rodando por estas partes.

in the jade green
born of morning
the spirals and blues
of fusion comes in
loud and clear
through radio waves
and camera lens

stretching eyes
must focus
on the shine of grass
not the harassment
or the twisting of minds
into believing in a reality
a mere copy of a life

Los indios entre
nosotros
con los rostros de otros
tiempos
que existen en estos
saben

truths are turned
inside out
bar codes and flag wave
slogans tattooed
on tongues pierced in two
they push on our images
to make them lies
their lies dirty truths

in this copy of real life
a fake freedom fighter
is one who stole his title and
fights for the rich against
those who have only stones
to throw against arsenals
designed
to blow us all away

what's wrong with this picture
when a *Con* can be called
a revolutionary and a
Revolutionary
painted a Dictator

haters know
how to twist language
and knives in backs
of once allies
after they're no longer useful
are made out to be the bad guys

corporate media
slur campaigns
strip leaders clean
of hero status
waltz them through
kangaroo courts
before doing away
with them for good

the demon people
would have us believe
that all they do

is in the name
of democracy
or Making America Great Again

code words
for stripping us
of all of our human rights
and for raping the earth
even further

some days
we have no hope
people self-medicate
just to cope
others write letters
make calls
to congress
sign petitions
vote

some of us
take to the streets
let our voices be heard loud
we Stand!
we Resist!
we Protect
earth for all our survival!

for now rain continues ...
as we in the struggle
as our world moves on
earth shifts her plates
maybe waits
to shake us all off
her back

Patents on Life

la Selva Lacandona
Chiapas
where green and red nations
are still free
in that place of heart
where the last virgin
rainforest lives
the rapists come
with their global concerns
raised in their greedy fist
like a flag or a hard on

in the deepest recesses
of an emerald green forest
on most days the rain falls
in big drops
for the better part
of afternoons
sometimes
there is a fine mist
24-hours a day
for weeks at a time
the tender buds
of new life
plants that breathe
the planet clean
are still being born

without the trees
there can be no rain
which is stored
in the clouds
in the leaves

of giant ancestor trees
that telegraph
the water needs
of earth's children
of all life

bio-prospecting
the last gold
bio-genetic plunder
and deforestation
trades of the Termite People
who puts patents
on our corn and rice
then charge farmers
for growing gifts
raised from the earth
as if they'd discovered it
lay their claim
like they did
on Turtle Island
which for millenniums
belonged to the people

the next ploy
will be patents on human life
then they'll charge mothers
for giving birth
after they're children born new
as tender shoots of maíz
peek their heads out
from the rich red earth
of mothers

we must remember
our original imperative
the divine messages
embedded in the crowns
of our own heads and
like the headdress
of Quetzalcoatl
with it we feed
our spirit selves
the lifeblood and
knowledge of the ages
we will not only survive
we will thrive

¡Que Viva La Vida!

Most Precious Twin

feathered serpent
riding wind
black beard *Ehecatl*
god of twins
benevolent father
you shed your own blood
onto ancestor bones
so that human
resurrection could begin

a wind jewel
fashioned from
a conch shell
around your neck and
jaguar bonnet
adorns your head
sharp bone pierces
your *nahualli's* heart
the royal green sacrifice
of your *quetzal* bird
born in fish deeps
you a child of the old ones
your dream that separates
night from day

Venus rising
on the morning horizon
great priest
our lord of penitence
rainclouds and sky
hold up the heavens
hold us
in your
cupped hands

Morning Star

spider   climbs   the horizon slowly

crawling   its way to evening

star's trajectory   force   invisible   nobility   cry

blades

           holding gods

                    at bay

return

the day   or we shoot   arrows

dipped   azul   our glyph   for Venus   holding

a scythe   say   what shall I sacrifice   today

some flesh will do

for now   we ride west   sinking into salty azure seas
once

you cut someone   deep   the itch never heals

a pearl of you   lodged   under skin

The Energies ~ Oshun and Xochiquetzal

Oshun or Osun, is the archetype of femininity and is associated with beauty, diplomacy, love, sensuality, peace and prosperity. But because she is the embodiment of femininity, or is all female, what is oftentimes overlooked, especially by people who don't really understand the feminine or its place in the world, is that she is one of the most powerful Orisha – a true force to be reckoned with.

In primordial times Oshun was the only female energy sent by Olodumare to accompany the first Irunmole to create the earth. The male energies were none too happy with her presence but soon learned that without Oshun nothing was going to happen. She reminds us that without the feminine there is no balance and without balance there is no earth, no creation, and no existence.

Oshun lives in the earth's sweet waters and is considered the holder of fertility. She is an expert at getting what she wants with her extreme intelligence and sweetness; her energy helps us overcome the most difficult of endeavors. Her stories teach us about satisfaction, joy, and delight. She is a master in the magical arts and is chief council member in matters pertaining to the delivery of justice.

The part of the body that pertains to her is the abdominal area, also blood, and other bodily fluids. She is invoked in matters concerning love and relationships, money, and the conception of children.

River rocks, gold or brass jewelry, fans, mirrors; peacock feathers and the colors golden-yellow, amber, and clear represent her. Her number is 5. Her favorite flower is said to be the sunflower. Honey, and pumpkins, are a few of the offerings made to her.

Xochiquetzal is the archetype of the feminine, of the young woman at the height of her sexual power. In her aspect as the quintessential energy of love, she represents voluptuousness, sensuality, sexual desire and pleasure in general. Her name means Flower Quetzal (Plumage) or Precious Flower. She is referred to as the divine being of song, dance and sexual pleasure. Her ceremony is celebrated during the time of the Farewell to the Flowers festival, in which a feast is given to honor the flowers that will soon disappear because of the coming frost.

Xochiquetal is associated with corn and vegetation in general. The divinity of flowers and grains, she is the patroness of artists: painters, sculptors, silversmiths, embroiderers, weavers, scribes, and prostitutes.

In the codex Cospi (fig.8) she is portrayed as a warrior, which would coincide with the legend that, she was the first woman to ever die in battle. It is also said that Xochiquetzal was taken to the underworld by *Xolotl* who violated her. In another account she is said to have eaten forbidden fruit, which produced an aphrodisiac affect and she became the first female to submit to sexual temptation. She was then expelled from the realm of creation at which time the forbidden tree split in two and she transformed into *Ixnextli*, Ashes in the Eyes, which also means being blinded by crying. It is said that her pain at not being able to look into the sky where she once lived, is why humans cannot look directly into the sun.

Xochiquetzal's flower is the *cempazuchitl*. Her image is made of wood in the shape of a young woman. A gold ornament placed over her mouth and a crown of red leather in the form of a braid is placed on her head. Bright green feathers adorn her headband.

For Oshun and Xochiquetzal in gratitude for love in all its beauty, pain, joy, and lament. For poetry and song ~ for brilliance in life.

For Protection

For ML

light travels fast through the gray shadow
of doubt and fear, you call me near and
wrap me in sweet basil leaves
hold me close and whisper
you tell me about fear and how it is all a lie
whisper in my ear and tell me how
real love never dies
tell me how time is elastic in the back-when
before this time moved on

burn the red copal for peace
burn the black copal to ward off hate, the evil

which you do not fear - because fear is a lie and
when we die, we only go home to the other side
that place, not sky, a thin gossamer veil divide

you swim with me in the dark emerald
pools of the way-back
the waterfalls singing behind us,
tell me how time stands still here
hold me with sweet basil smelling hands while
yellow eyed ocelotl spies us
from the green-yellow canopy

I leave lighter
with a gift from you
a rose quartz, in an ocher colored pouch
a hint of your brave heart, to wear next to mine

Siempre ~

Cantes a Palo Seco (a cappella)

yes, my
Gypsy dances
flamenco, fandangos.
and I am constantly dancing
on wind

she's from
a different drum.
wears those black strappy shoes,
slung back, tapping and stamping out
rhythm

her dance
not delicate
it cries out about life.
never whine, be a survivor—
like her

she breaks
down walls with her
feet. she beats injustice.
her hands clap-clap, away all our
sadness

Caló,
her old language,
a code of undertones.
honed across ages, echoes of
lost lands

her hands
instruments. she
can heal or kill at
will. depending on what you've done ~
deserve

she keeps
the beat, her feet
always fancy dancing.
her way of flying upright, while
dreaming

Anda
...lusia - walk
in the light, of your life
which is frightening enough, so shun
darkness

Rearranging
Reality
Straying
Away

Reality
Relativity
Away
Space

Relativity
Time
Space
Continuum

Circle
Web
Time
Wrinkle

Circles
Conjoined
Wrinkles
Purloined

Purloined
Dreams
Conjoined
Streams

Rivers
Stars
Dreams
Rearranging

The Distance of Love

her mouth
a wound
vermilion
a fire
smothered
by miles, years,
distances and
dreams deferred
desires stirred
by words
and images
when she heard
him say her name
enough times
to make her want
to come to him and only
then did they stand
faces turned into
the north wind
chanting their sin
of not having believed
enough in love
in the back when

Gitana's Prayer

in the convocation
of flamenco dancers'
percussive feet and
flaring skirts
Spanish guitars tweak
the indigo blue night's
summer star's heat
and in the light of fire
of fires she prays you
twirl her to rivers edge
singing an Arab's
North African song
to dance for the mother
who birthed her
already whole and
hungry to live

Parallel Universes

the rouge of camellias
their cinnamon scented faces
upturned towards coral light
our synchronous vibrations
reflected in this wholeness
where we are but a stitch
in the fine mesh
of creation's time

in a parallel universe
you and I have danced
this back and forth before
we have taken our love far
in all directions
as far as it will go
at once and never

again is often better
because by then
the rough edges
of youth are smoothed
as the peaks of proud mountains
are ground down by four winds

the plague of humanness
is striving for someone
else's idea of perfection or
not understanding the need
of becoming better humans
every day our flower faces
turned towards the light

Ololodi

for peace

once
a beautiful woman   stripped herself
of dress and veil   she mounted
a white war horse   bareback
and entered   the battlefield
very slowly   her beautiful long mane
flowing down   all around her small
delicate body   like the ripples of
a mighty river   a sight never
before seen   in a camp of blood
and carnage   some men stared
others stopped   to see why
the grunts and screams   had diminished
slowly   one by one   all the astonished
warriors   turned to   behold her
they put down   all their weapons
and all their shields   only then
was there peace

In the Pact of Closed Mouths

in the pact of closed mouths
we hurt no one with fire
tongues are kept chained

birds pull the cool breeze
along on their wings ~
singing in arms of North wind

a lake formed there
between lavish breasts
sweet a pleasant essence

thighs the goddess kind
ample and giving like earth
sculpted surrender

new moon knows the truth
all that hurt locked inside you
hiding behind words

rain blessed us big
parched and cracked we sing our thanks
we beg her to stay

complicated life
gets in the way ~ having
needs of a wild nature

stream of consciousness
empties into a blue lake
waits to be written

your name stained my lips
indelible it slips out
whenever I speak

all my wild horses
galloped through deep sleep
thundering your name

tiny bit of night
escaped sun's rays rising
savored in dark mouths

drowsiness flowers
follow me into my bed
ready to bloom sleep

bitter day's hot breath
beat down on tired stooped backs
dogs howling for rain

in summer's claws
we cry to be released
from heat's cruel clutches

language in dark eyes
deciphered by keen lovers
turns to caresses

promise me love
an entire life even
if for one day

all the naysayers
living inside my head
say leave the past buried

the morning came late
she's waits in the garden
and talks to the sky

forget you never
forever ended sooner
than eternity

maps on emerald leaves
point to far flown directions
of your want for me

never want to wake
from this dream of you ~
loving me in farthest night

my liberation
is the same as my prison
loving you

an ocean tattooed
blue on her fluid body
a dance for the moon

give me love
your sex flowers in my hand
ripen lusciously

my existence
your ardent lips on mine
consumes me

all this talk of love
knowing so well in our minds
how much pain it brings

feels good to hunger
to really feel desire
instead of empty

desire fire
hunger to be consumed
burns a bright red-blue

raven's cawing
sounds of blue sky beckoning
cloud's murky darkness

rumblings of rain
throaty noise on rainclouds edge
promising downpours

text messages sent
might as well be smoke signals
to digital voids

air's hot dragon breath
makes one want to slither
under a cool rock

red-tailed hawk circles
she can't wait to share dinner
searches for her mate

noche
luna llena
de ti

drunk summer slumber
dreaming frozen fjords winter
storms kicking up winds

ancestors
wildflowers on Spring roadsides
bloom again

astral bodies
vibrating sound ~ kissing
your unconscious hand

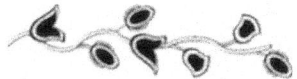

The Energies ~ Oya and Tlazolteotl

Oya is one of the greatest sorceresses of the Yoruba pantheon and has close ties to the ancestors. She is guardian, or gatekeeper of the cemetery, and is said to be the only Orisha who is not afraid to face Iku – death. The wind in all its manifestations, and air, even in its form of, "our first and last breath," is said to belong to Oya. As does the clash of cool and hot air, which produces the fire of the lightning, seen before the thunderclap. As female warrior she represents the courage to face and manage instant and sometimes devastating change with the alpha-female quality of fierce strength combined with the wherewithal and intelligence to find nonviolent solutions to problems. Those with her energy are strong, assertive, courageous, independent, and always willing to take risks – especially to help others.

Oya in her earthly incarnation was called *Iyansan*, mother of nine, though it is said that before she birthed her nine children she had problems with fertility, and because of this she went to consult the sacred Ifa Oracle. She was instructed through Orunmila to do ebo, sacrifice, and was advised of the proper remedy to take in order to have children.

Oya is the master of change and as such is attributed with having the ability to shapeshift whenever necessary. She is the patron of the marketplace and the up and down nature of the wheel of fortune, and the winning and losing of fortunes. She is invoked in times of serious illness and when change is needed. It is however important to be specific as to the rapidity with which one would like to see that change happen because violent change can be very unsettling – to say the least.

One of her totems is the African buffalo. Her attributes include copper items, buffalo horns, bones, machetes, and masks. Oya's colors are vibrant and varied; she likes maroons, deep oranges, reds, and fabrics with multicolored patterns reminiscent of the varied flowers brought to the cemetery. Offerings include eggplant, dark grapes, pomegranates, plums, akara – bean fritters, and red wine. Her number is nine.

Tlazolteotl which means Eater of Filth, is also known as *Ixcuina*. She is considered to be a fertility and warrior goddess; known as the Patroness of Sex, and the Mistress of Spinning. Tlazolteotl as the devourer of sins (filth eater,) is said to consume the sins of the people when they confess them to her, usually at the time of their death. As Lady of healers and sorcerers, she has power over all forms of unclean behavior; she is the divinity of carnal matters, and able to test people by inciting illicit love affairs, and lust.

Tlazolteotl is regarded as an archaic representation of the great mother earth. In her aspect as mother of the energies *Teteoinan*, she is the patroness of midwife/healers who have the gift of divining with grains of corn. This form of divination goes hand in hand with healing methods that these women practice.

A major energy of the México, Tlazolteotl's ceremonies are held during the month That One Sweeps, *Ochiponiztli*. She is said to have appeared in four forms, which some speculate correspond to the phases of the moon. In one of the codices she is represented as a pregnant woman with her legs spread open in a birthing position.

She is usually depicted wearing a band of cotton on her headdress and a black tattoo covering her nose and mouth. She is also shown wearing symbols of the moon, and with a broom in hand indicative of change, and the sweeping away of filth or negativity from people's lives. Like Xochiquetzal, she is shown dressed in warrior gear.

For Oya and Tlazolteotl in gratefulness for learning how to embrace change as one should the wind, and for knowing that life cannot be beautiful without also being ugly.

Invocation for Tlazolteotl

in blue veils
of copal and cedar smoke
I salute you
oh mother of
the entrails of earth
carnal love
you ocelotl
slayer of sins
filth eater
I pray you
ravage sickness
drink acid rains
gift us
the unclouded waters
breathe in
all the loathsome air
send strong winds
end their obsession
the termite peoples
swallowing up
all that stands
in their path
help us your children
who suffer diseases
that devour hearts
hear our prayers
we whisper
our lives
to you

Ofrenda (Dos)

In an old sequoia circle
ringed in cool conjunction
a cacophony of voices
the hum of ruby throated
hummingbirds and
the loud croaks of frogs
performing their annual
mating rituals strong
as though selling snake-oil
or hawking their wares
in the market square
they croon their hearts out

while down below
in a stand of trees
people leave offerings
for the spirits of the forest
to honor their loved ones
at the feet of these ancient ones
there very thoughtfully placed
on chipped white porcelain plates
a variety of cooked grains, and other foods
red, black, and white beans in tiny burlap sacks
small cakes, a variety of fruits and root vegetables
miniature statues and all kinds of precious stones and rocks

once   someone left a very tiny fetus
wrapped in soft with cloth cradled
in a fine miniature woven tapestry
fastened secure with ribbon thin red leather straps
a sepia toned photograph of a very old,
but beautiful, grandmother and a note which said

I am so sorry dear grandmother
that you did not make it back
I shall pray that you will come again and
that next time you will take that precious
breath of life and stay with us for
many years to come.
I shall have the jeweler fashion you
a special silver bracelet with bells,
a sounding spell, to keep you
from going back to the other side… so soon
I love you.

purple, orange, and red lollipops
fashioned into an extra sweet bouquet
black, red, yellow, and white prayer ties
strung in the trees flutter like tiny butterflies
a ball of real cotton stuck
with ten shiny silver needles
in a basket woven like a nest and
plates of sumptuous food on
chipped white china plates

are all left here at this ancestor gate

On the Veranda

tonight when I sat in the dark
eating your *sandia* heart

while scanning the moonless sky
for a trace of one blue-bright star

that gleam in your obsidian eyes
as I spit out those black seeds far

was the only glimpse
of heaven

Wounds

she was born
from a wound
into a wounded
world wedged
into a space
so small
where all her
people did not fit
rendered
non-people
or nondescript
mere farm implements
or other such tools
where the dollar and
cruel power ruled
no kindness
for her kind
just more of
the same
wounds

Deep Breathing

the light comes in the window
different now,
so much brighter and
clouds do have lustrous linings
that bring living rain
prayed for, by those
who still know rain prayers and
how to make the frogs sing for more.
there is a different sound
just on the edge of all that is said,
all that I say now
has a different feeling,
like hope that the end of the world
isn't eminent.
there is no distant star
about to burn up
into our atmosphere, or
crash into the planet. and that
those crazy people, with the power to do so,
won't push that last button
any minute
just because they can.
the moon kisses me in sleep
leaves me dreams of the Milky Way and
all the ancestors who've gone on
who care for the generations coming back
whisper messages in the dark
hoping someone is listening.
I breathe deeper knowing
you are there, that you see
who I am now, so far away
from yesterday

'Yansan 9

fury
of beating wings.
whirlwinds stirred turbulent.
spiraling rataplan, squalling
power

mantled
tempest tilting.
traces of copper coiled
augured chaos, the winds telling.
let go

let go

let go

let　it　go

Cuando Muere La Tarde ~

preciso instante
el día y la noche
los mundos indefinidos

inmóvil y fríos
lluvia de estrellas
los rayos de luz

agujeritos en la manta
de lapislázuli
mis trajes de noche

en mundos irreales
llenos de ángeles
escondidos

y siendo guerrera
canto una flor por todos
los que mas amo

con vuelco en mi corazón
una lengua dulce
una paz dulce

When Afternoon Dies~

precise instant
the day and night
world's undefined

cold and unmovable
a rain shower of stars
rays of light

little holes
in my lapis lazuli shawl
my evening clothes

for unreal worlds
full of hidden angels
and being a warrior

I recite a flower
for all those
I love most

with tumble in my heart
a sweet tongue
a sweet peace

Body Oracle

read this body   in etched   tattoos   my codex

doesn't pollute   too many words   overrated   our silence obsolete

essential   a ballet   walk away

word bullets   pulp chatterers   ask yourself   who reads what why?

un red   the web   caught up futures

naysayers   eclipses   digital books

codices   codes   not Morse   binary

is there   something to say   some cut lines

in their skin   is it a sin   or a sign   of some kind

others draw lines in ocher dirt   millennium messages   told from

mouths

of seeds   and shells   spiders   the star webs

read ourselves   your heart could   tell you plenty
and

your body's big enough every square inch   could tell your story

of this or that hurt   how many years [have] you had   those scars?

Copper Hands

wrinkled brown copper hands
in the red earth planting
the blood colored dahlias
she is famous for
the petal arrows
direct her loved ones South
where the ancestors came from
all her babies and their babies
placentas are buried there
under cherry trees that blossom in
a sweet produce
luscious vermilion fruit

some are buried under the Indian apples
the pomegranates with their bitter sweet
blood seeds
a passion fruit people tend to discount
papery thin skin   tough enough
to chamber a crimson heart
not that easy to enter or to get out of
its juicy stain indelible

in her youth she was a *guerrera*
with *el rojo y negro*
always in forefront
ready to give her life
she gave up her girly and frivolous things
like her coral-red nail polish
fire engine red lipstick and
her biggest sacrifice
those red strapless
patent-leather spiked heels
all for *La Causa*!

she was a firebrand
no one had a sharper tongue
could cut a man to the quick
or kiss him deep until he thought
he'd suffocate in what felt like rage or lust
but wasn't
she was good at leaving too
better alone than in bad company
it's what she'd always taught her girls
not her boys they lived leaving

Emiliano her oldest
could run before he walked
went to Vietnam and stumbled
straight into death
now he's buried in the *maizal*
when she'd asked
the powers that be
for permission
to bury her son there
on their ancestral lands
they'd said that people
couldn't be planted
straight into the ground
like some kind of seed
so, she lets them think
her boy still rests
in that gvmnt issued box
the Army put him in
which sits at the bottom
of a deep dark-blue hole
in that cemetery
with rows and rows
of sad white crosses

one night she took her brothers
out to that graveyard and they dug her boy up.
wrapped him tightly in a blessed Pendleton blanket
lowered him gently into a ritual resting place
her baby back in the mother's red womb
under the blue corn field

tending the corn her favorite task
from the time of the tender green shoots
to the long days of the tall sturdy stalks
she gets to talk with her oldest offspring
she gathers the golden corn pollen
saves it for the birthing ceremonies
of all her descendants
the first gift placed on their sweet
salmon tongues
it blesses their miniature heads,
hearts, hands and the bottoms
of their tiny red feet
so that they will grow grounded

this sweet pollen is also gifted
for the puberty ceremonies of the newly bloomed
showered down like golden grains of sand
on the heads of all the young women
of her *familia* who run the red foot race
of time into maturity

her brown-copper hands carried boycott and *huelga* signs
she sought justice for all the generations, later she
buried her losses then seeded and grew food and medicine
to weave love for her past and future
to bless all the clans ~ Siempre!

Days of the Dead

for Hawk

summer yesterdays, all green and heat are gone
today it's all gray fog and cold breeze
brown, orange, and yellow leaves swirl
around on these urban streets on All Hallows Eve
teen goblins and adolescent geeks tug at younger siblings
– dressed as all kinds of little creeps –
they scurry up and down the streets, and we hear,
let's keep up or we won't get any treats
the haunting goes down until long after dark
'til the city streets empty of all those looking for sweets

en los campos, las familias will arrange flowers and feasts
for our *muertos* who have long since left this beast
this is the night before they make their return
we prepare to honor them with celebration and song
for the adults: *los tamales* of ripe, or new green corn,
mole, atole, arroz y frijoles for *los angelitos*
offerings in clay cups filled with fruit,
con chocolate, pan de muerto, calaveras de azúcar y luz

tomorrow at dusk when the church bells ring
we will march to the *camposanto* and make offerings
las veladoras will shine in last light of day
with the smell of copal y *cempasúchil* flower petals to guide the way
we are of the old though we become part of the new
and though the bloods mixed with earth remain but a few
we must always remember to honor our dead
for it is they who will greet us with open arms
when our living days are through

The Energies ~ Yemaya and Chalchiuhtlicue

Yemaya is a major Orisha, considered to be the divine mother of life and of many of the Orisha. It is said that she is the owner of all the waters. In the diaspora she is represented by the ocean – which, as a fundamental life source covers more than 70 percent of the world's surface. In Yemaya's manifestation as Olokun, and some say in androgynous form, s/he is represented by deepest ocean.

As a primordial divinity of the seas and moon, she is the archetypal mother and her energy is that of quintessential nurturer, providing stability and sustenance to earth's children. She is overly generous and forgiving but like the ocean, when she's had enough of people taking advantage, or of being wantonly disobedient, her fury can be fierce. Yemaya, who is said to be the owner of intelligence and of the collective unconscious, is also a grand sorceress who holds ancient wisdom and the secrets hidden by the ocean. She is invoked by pregnant women to aid in the birthing process and by anyone needing stability on the earth.

Her symbols include any treasures returned from the sea, such as shells, stones, or glass; silver objects, such as the *abebe* – a silver fan, or silver jewelry. Her colors are blue, white and clear. Yemaya's number is 7 and some of her offerings include watermelon, plantain chips, pork rinds, and blue and or white flowers.

Chalchiuhtlicue She of the Jade Skirt, is the divinity of terrestrial waters, and of the living waters or those that flow. She is the archetype of the grand nurturing mother; she who nurtures the people so that they can multiply. She is metaphorically pictured as such in the Codex [Borgia] – nursing humankind. Chalchiuhtlicue is known as She of the Sea and Lakes, She of springs and Rivers, Jade Skirt, She Who Was the Water. Also known as *Xoxouhqui Ihuipil*, or *Xoxouhqui Icue*, meaning Her Skirt is Green.

Chalchiuhtlicue is also venerated during the birthing process. When a child is born, a special ceremony is officiated over by the midwife. She shouts war cries in honor of the battle fought by mother and baby during the course of the birth, and in honor of the mother as a triumphant warrior for having captured a baby. In the ritual bathing of the newborn, the midwife washes the child and tells him/her the story of their birth, she then invokes Chalchihuitlicue and entrusts the child to her, she who is responsible for carrying them in her arms on the path of their destiny.

In Chalchiuhtlicue's aspect as a water energy, she represents the font of life in the highest degree, but equally as important is her ability to purify, rejuvenate and give new life. The people, with the intention of ridding themselves of undesirable energies, have habitually practiced ritual bathing to reemerge cleansed of negativity and of certain illnesses. She is naturally considered a divinity of fertility and fecundity because of the planet's need of water for life to thrive. Chalchiuhtlicue is the patron saint of the sea and of the people who make their living from the water. Shrines made to her are built near oceans, streams, aqueducts, or irrigation ditches.

It is said that Chalchiuhtlicue loves flowers, which are offered to her along with special cotton headdresses made in her honor. Her attire consists of paper ornaments painted blue and white; her headpiece has tassels, which hang down either side of her face. It was not uncommon to see her pictured wearing a representational mask of Tlaloc, the Rain God, which is considered to be her brother or her husband, depending on the legend. She is thought to manifest in water vortexes.

Dedicated to Yemaya and Chalchihuitlicue, with deep respect for all that motherhood, birth, rebirth and regeneration does for our souls and the planet; and special gratitude for water, which is life.

Diosa

a galaxy of bright stars
adorned her swaying black night skirt
with silvery threads of moonlight
sister spiders embroidered lightning bolt and web patterns
on the summer sky blue huipil she wore
a garland of jet snakes dancing about her neck and chest
radiant face of a billion lives enclosing eyes of fire and ice
full rust colored lips, which break into abalone shell teeth smiles
from time to time. hair the color and smell of wood pitch
from which all life flows crowning her head a hoop of white roses
reminds her that she is the queen of the universe

at first her planet was cold and still
then she learned that with steps her feet would take
small impressions on the surface she could create
blue oceans, rushing rivers streams or emerald lakes
crystalline water, liquid stars
all this made her happy
on the planet her breath she would blow
from this, tall green grasses, lush prairies, and
marshes began to grow this gift of life she'd known
now she was generating existence all on her own
this made her happy

in clay the same copper color as her skin
with outstretched arms and hands into her world she'd
sculpt deep canyons, mighty mountains, mesas and hills
at night she'd dream the flowers
delicate orchids, snowy larkspur, freesia, Indian pipe, lupine,
calla and tiger lilies, marigolds, desert sunflowers
bathing in their fragrance slowly she'd awaken
with ample bouquets clutched to her breasts

years passed, her home had grown she traveled
from the jeweled jungles and rainforests
to the ocher deserts and jade valleys
all teeming with her luscious fruits yet
she sensed something was missing
all that lived and breathed on her world
only moved in the winds and rains she'd bring
she wanted beings like herself to laugh and sing with

Diosa had created a world full of life but try as she might
she could not find a way to create an end to her loneliness
one day as she wept a serpent from the necklace she wore
bathed in her tears awoke and slid away, the little snake
could not believe her good fortune as she crawled and
marveled at the wide world around her
happy to have such a wondrous existence
as she slithered about and realized
that one day soon she would become a mother

sister spiders came down from the heavens
suspended from silvery threads
they wrapped the mother serpent in a soft cocoon
in seven days the silky shell began to give way
from its opening came forth a column of deafening wind
a crack of lightning and clap of thunder in the blue-black sky
in the gales magnificent winged struggled to fly
on the ground in the rain turtles, lizards and
other crawlers scurried for new cover
there were majestic four-legged,
and insects of every kind

Diosa saw everything
and could not believe her eyes
she sang a song of thanks and
praise to all her new relatives

that night she dreamt
of exquisite beings like
those she'd never seen
two legged like herself
and though they couldn't fly
they could think,
speak, laugh, sing and cry

when she awoke
lying next to her
on the ground
she found two babies swaddled
in the satiny leaves
of one of her giant trees

Bella Luna

Void of Course

jaguars the tzitzimime come to cover the night sky in their black shiny coats the eye cannot see what is concealed but one can feel the spirits whispering the sounds of what is needed to win this battle of jaguar's night and eagle's light both a half of the balance

New

there is a hint a curved scratch of light on a backboard of blackest night infinity hurling through endless space silence the color of light determined reflections objects divinely placed in perfect symmetry to cause upsets in the universal balance of nothingness
made chaos solid mass in tiny crystals flowered life and the stars that burn hot are water blue flames fly high red shooting their wad towards planets at the speed of light that's gone out before we were ever born to die in a flick of an eyelash or beat of a heart it's what we see as wrong destiny played out for all life though energy is eternal and we are unmade into star dust to seed the future

Half-full

a seed seeding into fruit movement an expansion of light incremental shedding on darkness there is no room for frightening realizations the dark side of the womb holds surprises ruined by precipitated revelations the unknown and the hidden until it's time like wine must ripen its bloom bursting first nose and lips then on tip of tongue spinning its road's stories into realizations a bloom's maturation nectar takes a course the gods set forth the invisible slope or is it a silvery rope with which they pull the orb forward into fullness hope is an opening on doubt a widening to future possibilities once overshadowed by the darkness of wallowing in the past but change comes in
different phases even it may be lost to the naked or half- closed eyes

Timpani

the shining   the rapture
cold blue when it's a twin sensation that generations have marveled at since the
beginning when the first gods met in total darkness it was decided someone had
to jump into the fire the first would be a flame to provide all life-light for
eternity the One who self-immolated became the mighty red sun rising proud
across the sky dying daily for humankind the one who followed who leaped
and threatened to become another ball of fire in heaven equal to no other so, the
gods grew alarmed and quickly threw handfuls of gray ashes into the bright fire's
face   smothering it some before the sphere could rise to the sky in only a
muted shawl of flame   and when this dimmed pocked mark face smiles full
down not once but twice in one-month people are amazed it is all the rage as
it happens only once in a blue inspiring an overflow of love at this dual ripening
loved most is the huge golden one we view as pregnant with the harvest of hope
and promise of abundance   and there are more words to describe plenty than
you can hold in your hands like liquid silver flowing through your fingers you
can only catch what is yours to have and that is decided in heaven

Half Empty

in a half shell toss what is lost in this hanging dimensional by not viewing the
whole you miss what is shaded by the naked eye *Coyolxauhqui* drawn and
quartered by her own brother Huitzilopochtli who angrily tossed her skyward
she is now but an orb of silver   a goddess seen only in slices by the world her
devotees painted blue bathe naked in the shadows of her white light lamina   the
Centzonhuitznáhuac her other brothers slaughtered too by the hummingbird
prince sit small in the night sky twinkling back other timelines and stories of
bloodless battles when the people counted coup on each other and only spilled
the sacred chalchíhuatl the precious liquid four times a year in honor of the
blessed for what was lost was found in the sacrifice and new spheres opened up
to the believers though in the shiny green feathered blood-thirsters

new world order these were not the dreamkind   but rather nightmare realities that left ones lost and aching for their own familiar terrain a balance between the light and the darkness which frightened only with a frequency   that was predictable or at minimum manageable through the manipulation of prayer offerings and songs flowers put towards this vision of a wider world   with as little suffering as possible   with less greed to feed the negative past

Five Senryū

~ an offering to Ocean~

on wings of ocean
water gives life or destroys ~
they were carried skyward

ocean endless
with no bottom to speak of
she cannot be blamed

for mysteries of life
painful as they are deep
clouds without answers

mighty ships sink as
if gravity were no more
a chasm

earth-water fissures
a breach in reality
our safety lost

In Between Sleep and the Light

new dreams
desecrated,
hollowed out. ringing on
the fried side. midnight calling too
early

filling
rooms, clear aqua
reflecting near perfect
an inner cease to feel. pain in
dawn sky

she swims
peaceful. knowing
she breathes underwater.
her mother taught her while birthing
fishes

wishes
are woken dreams.
not broken by sticks or
bones. crippled by wicked spirits
on whims

evil
launched by adults
who throw their children's red
hearts as grenades. and pretend they
are grown

sown in
ocean sands, long
fought out. in that constant
back and forth of salty stones. washed
shore-ward

and so
it goes nightly,
counting of sheep or clouds.
then, rouse the sandman to join — the
sleepless

Chalchihuitlicue's Story

After the first birth breath bursts forth from the bud and
the sweet yellow corn pollen is placed in her sprout pink mouth
the jade green ritual bath is poured and in swirling whispers
the midwife to her spirit lovingly washes the new vessel
which is her body and tells of time long before this one
long before the embryonic waves held her in her mother's
red womb for this symbiotic journey here and as if possessed
in a reedy voice she cries

when I was the queen of Nahui atl 4 waters
I destroyed the world
enveloping it in a watery grave
for humans disobeyed and
I sunk them under my great wings
for fifty-two years until it was decided enough
was enough and I receded the wild jade-green waters

I who give life
can take it in the same way
at the mouth where the river is born
source of all life flows forth and back again
I am She of the Jade Skirt
who born fully formed
emerged to give birth to all

who must remember always
destiny is chosen

oh little bird you must learn
to see both front and back and that
red is red and black is black

Mother of the fishes

the tip of her crown
Northern Star

her ebony hair reflects
black the night

her eyes bound tight
in a starry clad scarf

so we will not see
her eternal vision which blinds

fiery red lips line
summer's setting sun

dusty rose nipples
her coral reefs jet skyward

life's nectar   oceans
flowing from her breasts

in time with her swaying hips
she stirs the waves

dance out and back again
our bodies crave the rhythm of her tides

La Llorona's Sacred Waters

she holds us in the wing of her arm and
all we hear at the edge of the world is
las ranas crying   *perdiendo se gana*
perdiendo se gana perdiendo se…
for our survival she throws us
into the watery vortex we are hurled
left to swirl down to where we all began
and return again in the ancestor's
children's children's children

sometimes
a desperate mother
must return herself and
her children
to the blue void
where the waters
are not still not rushing
but a soothing place
to rock her babies back
to the big sleep
their souls to keep
to plant them as seeds
once again
in a watery tomb
the universal womb
from where all life springs
a better place
without suffering
no longer sought
in a cruel world who cares not
about future generations and
merely wants to use them
as tools to rule them

for their own motives
money or profit

we come in tiny writhing drops
into a sea of darkness swimming up
a perilous canal   a life journey
not to be stopped then a half of us
must penetrate the luminous calabash of life
to become whole   be born a higher form
we swim semi-conscious
in the briny waters and curve
of our mother's bright coral womb
we stew until done
then emerge but we surge and stop
which causes her much pain
at the same time joy
for that first communion
nine months earlier
resulted in an us
her new flower blooms
in a gush of holy water
we flow out
to greet the world
once again

Intervention of Angels

there are grandmothers
standing all around us
applauding and laughing
in sheer delight
they saw us together
in a long-ago dream
but how to get us
to see one another
took stars and blue sky
their tried and true schemes

I was going far away
forever from the pacific sea
it took opening a different door
so they could usher you in

now we hear heaven the music
reflected in our new rhythm
we go through the changes
one beat at a time

life is funny that way
you can think you know
what's right or what is up ahead
then the intervention of angels

can change the future simply
by two hands held in friendship
in flowers given freely
with full moons and sweet song

Of Sepia Toned Mysteries

her mother
a sepia toned woman
who always lost
lovely faced
a portrait of trouble
a nobody
someone loved
her language
the way she moved
a beautiful orchid
deep purple
the way the light
spread from her and
radiated outward
her image growing
trying to find love
she lost
from her own
mother
being gone –
alienated from her

her life
code words
written down
as letters
to get to numbers
the math of it all
the putting of two
and two together
getting jazz
or *corridos*
instead of simple
answers to questions

she didn't think
to ask

and jazz open
to all kinds of mystery
or interpretations
a kind of flesh
offering like flowers
cut and steeped
for strong tea
for listening to

y los corridos
stories of our pueblos
are warm scarves
to keep out the cold and
guard against the old
lies told over and over
that never become truths
because the people know
and sing truths of their own stories

her life is sewn together like
those scarves that keep
people warm and protected
she has no home
only deep roots and
distilled connections
she carries their essence with her
like her ancestors
around her neck on a silver chain
each one represented
by a charm that tell a story
of sepia skin
of life's journeys
of all the loves
of her life

Water Song

in our mother's red womb
we hear the voices
of ancestors we have been and
of those who shall become
our parents our family

mostly we hear her heart
in the waves of water
that encircle and cradle us
safely inside her sacred calabash
until we are ready to emerge
onto the shores of this next existence

we begin our lives
with that first drink
of her abundant richness
our mother's sweet - thin
sacred water the milky blue
of millenniums

we grow
knowing water is life
without it we do not survive
it is all life's birthright
water heals and cleanses us
the only liquid we need
to grow
life

The Energies ~ Shango and Huitzilopochtli

Shango the fourth warrior King of the Yoruba, immortalized as the divinity of thunder, is legendary among the Lucumi, and considered to be one of the most popular Orisha. Shango's thunderstorms though often violent, bring a purifying effect to the earth. His energy has to do with the gift of speech as it relates to honesty, justice, peace, and understanding. These attributes support the skill of master diplomat and charismatic leader. In people, the negative flipside can manifest itself as the liar, braggart, and egotist who will not let anyone get a word in edgewise.

Shango is an Orisha of many gifts and is said to have loved music, especially drumming, dance, and having fun in general. The sacred bata drums, which are played in tribute to the Orisha, belong to him. He is an expert herbalist, highly skilled in divination and magic, and is invoked to deal with issues of justice and setting things right in people's lives.

It is said that Shango's close relationships with other Orisha included only Esu-Elegua and Orunmila. His three wives were Oba, Oya, who had also been Ogun's wife, and Oshun. He is the protector of the *Ibeyi* – the sacred twins – and of children in general.

His colors are red and white, his number is 6 and his symbols include the double-edged ax, the sword, and the mortar and pestle. Some of his offerings include cornmeal mush with okra, red apples, prickly pears, and red wine.

Huitzilopochtli at the time of the conquest of Mexico, was known as the deity of war, son of *Coatlicue*, the earth mother, and the principal divinity worshiped by the Mexica people. He embodied the sun, the special guardian of *Tenochtitlan*. This deified ancestral warrior-hero, was the preeminent historical protector of the Mexica-Aztec people. His temple constructed next to that of Tlaloc, venerated to bring the rains, at the Templo Mayor (Main Pyramid), was the center of ceremonial activities and of sacrifices of prisoners captured by Mexica warriors in the Flowery Wars.

Huitzilopochtli may have been born on Coatepec Mountain, near the city of Tula. He is considered to be an incarnation of the sun that struggles with the forces of night to maintain life on the planet earth. He gained major importance in the worship of the Mexica people as he is credited with inducing them to migrate from their ancestral homeland in Aztlan, where it is said they were poor and struggling. They began the long wanderings, which brought them to the valley of Mexico where they prospered into one of the most powerful nations of their time. It is said that Huitzilopochtli was little known before the Mexica's coming to Mexico.

According to legend, *Coatlicue*, also mother of the moon or *Coyolxauhqui*, and the 400 stars called the *Centzonhuitznahuac*, became pregnant with Huitzilopochtli when a ball of green feathers fell to her breasts while she was sweeping. *Coatlicue's* children became jealous of her "illegitimate" pregnancy and plotted to kill her. During his birth, Huitzilopochtli used "serpent of fire," the sun's rays to defeat the moon and stars. Every day the battle continues between day and night. The Mexica saw the sunrise as a daily victory over the forces of darkness. Huitzilopochtli is said to reside in seventh heaven, which is represented by the color blue. His temple on the great Pyramid in Tenochtitlan was called *Lihuicatl Xoxouqui*, or Blue Heaven. His image is a wooden statue carved to look like a man seated on a blue wooden bench in the form of a liter. His headdress is shaped into a hummingbird beak made of gold. The feathers adorning the headdress, a beautiful green. In his left hand he holds a shield, with five bunches of white feathers in the form of a cross. Although Huitzilopochtli is worshipped often during the entire México year, *Panquetzaliztli*, the feast honoring the raising of banners, is generally thought to be his major yearly feast.

For Shango and Huitzilopochtli who embody the essence of warriors and remind us of the importance of having as big a heart as you do courage. Without great love, defense of a peoples can become the oppression of others.

Dreaming Huitzilopochtli

buzzing   elongated necks   fragrant

lusting   precious   liquid   crown of calyx   lobes

la colorada   a calumet   calliope   trills

prayer   not sound   in white camisole   she eats   Indian
apples

and lets   drip   the crimson   scarlet rain

it dyes   these lips   camellias   in the garden   camouflage

a ruby   chested messenger   calls on wings   in the
window

juice is   sweet   a strange fruit's   not   understood

olorosas   *y*   tendertipped

blooms burst   forbidding and   *o mi ocelotl*

yo comprendo esta cantata   Spring   is finally here

Chocolate
chile
aguacate
calabaza
cacahuate

papas
tomate
elote
frijoles

más que oro
se llevaron los españoles

Kolonial Legacy

Landscape chiseled in   blood   Speed of sound   cut paws

non-native analysis   justified murder   we say no   this country

cold blooded   their shadows.   still walk   waiting to jump

the unsuspecting   to avenge their dead full-motion light   wild guesses

anagrammed hangman   won't bite   hermit champions   addicted to

conundrums   fleshing out bodies   to build their own   home on the

range   brain doodling lives   collapse in   on blue

light specials   feel the power   carved free hand   the last

word   black box fails to say   serrated edge

plunged deep enough   but it cannot penetrate

the vidiot inferno   still   the shadows know

Blue Hummingbird On The Left

premeditated　　　　　　harmonies　　spaces between the sound louder

part of the pattern　　　gardens　　　flowers　　stuck in pots

shiny-red ooze　　　　　　sunrise eye exists

petals stem　root rot　　　y tree　　　　a selfish love　　solitary

peninsula blank　　　　　　windows blink cloudy

rivers run across the　　sung aloud　　　　　cielos

life blood　　　sucking　　　hummingbird prince　　the big sun

suffering

smitten　　　　　　mourning　　　　　started

summer breeze　　　　kissed

seemingly swans are still　　eagle's wings aéreo plane

an ecstasy circus　　at river's edge　　　　　　spotted dogs bark

at their reflection　beneath　　　the wind　　colors　　salt and bones darken

sea　　　　　　sound melodies of rain wake

　　　　　　　　　　　　　　　　the sleeping

Six in the Mix

coral reef broken
and split pomegranates
ruby bejeweled bones

light in burnt shadows azure
boat passing sunset cools
still the scorched day

her hips slingshot moves
on dark beach belly dancing
to season's last breaths

map's myths ululant
seashore see-sawing dark blues
autumn storm looming

time bent back on itself
winding clocks crisscrossed
stars grazing at strand's edge

compassing the world
beyond land's pull of cellos
in wild indigo

The Blues for Saxophone

1
two-toned
blue midnight
before, after and 'round—
sax sounds shimmer down sorry stairwells
wishing

2
no one
was home to care.
delicious the solitude
of condemned buildings waiting—
to hear

3
reedy
and haunting high,
the blue notes colliding
in the emptiness of times past—
pushing

4
out-breath
breeding bellows
sounding like cries delight,
the space between pleasure and pain—
raining

5
showers
of sound sighing
through brassy pipe, calling
ancients their music mimicking—
voices

Transformations

our sacrifices
are no longer human
some are home-made
drums carved from
sacred trees
uniting rhythm worlds
in transition give birth
to something new
our herb man knows
a few ploys
he no longer does
ventriloquists' tricks
idols behind altars
a *golpe de Santo* and
amulets for protection
save lives
but to learn
you must live it
beads are a give-away
straw mat obeisance
life's map on your head
rain river ocean
our holy water
nature's baptisms

Prickly Pear Hearts

not a coincidence
I was born on a rainy day
after a long night and
from way inside her
I could hear her praying
with breath and teeth
cursing the day they met

she was all of ten
he was thirteen
said *see her*
she'll be mine
but she was not the kind
for marriage and kids
can't put a hold on the wind

they called her mustang wild
said she was wild boar mean
at five years old she snapped
a few baby chick's necks
just to prove them right
but he wasn't fooled
by her surly exterior
he'd hear her nights singing
her voice a cup of sadness
echoed in a valley
of migrant workers
always leaving

to roam endless roads
that destined sorrow
her voice rang out
wishes of different tomorrows

and in that there was hope
a heart always singing for more

to him she was a prickly pear
with needle sharp thorns
that protected her
soft and golden heart
and for years she kept
him at a distance
whenever he passed her house
she'd rolled her eyes
call to him *jackrabbit*
or *stupid silly grin*

but he was true in his pursuit
and when they grew older
at dances, he'd ask her out
on the floor and she'd oblige
but hide any delight
as they whirled and twirled
stepping in time all time
future and past or so it seemed
they would enter a dream
spiral and couldn't stop dancing
until the evening's music stopped

then she would wake from the trance
act angry at him for having held her up
from dancing with others
but in these dance dreams
other lives took over
because ancestor souls never die
are reborn in future generations

at all the dances from then on

they'd become ribbons of sky
wind themselves around each other
and dance dance dance
until they were like one soul
and the people were surprised
gossiped about this strange turn
of events many said
that happened out of the blue
must be brujería
but he knew
that what he'd felt
on the very first day they met
all those years earlier
was true
he'd always known she would
change her mind about him
after all he was hers
and she his
they each other's destiny

but after a few months
tears ran down both
their cheeks
as they said their goodbyes
but he vowed never
to let her love go
he left for Korea
a lock of her night-black hair
in his heart pocket
for luck and for future

It's no sin

to be an *Indio*
that survived
no crime to refuse
to sit around
pretending
or act dimwitted
drinking ourselves to
death on Colt 45's
thinking about all we lost
all that was sacred to us
tossed away so easily
because the value
is on unnatural things
money paid
for manufactured misery
dizzying the masses
so they won't think
see the stink of waste
the chase for goods
causes dementia
many are so scared
they don't live in reality
instead are fed life
intravenously through TV and
corporate media news
those who claim to know
but only represent the interests
of the few and we are taught
to trust lies and liars more
than what's in our guts what our spirits
put right up in our faces traces of a past
still here mirroring a way out of
the *mitote* madness

Insomnia

for Angel

it was dark yes, almost
light and I was looking
at your side of the bed
it was empty again
I thought, I'm dreaming
but not knowing really

you're lost someplace between
here and there and I keep
dreaming you back in bed
on my side where you love to sleep
when I'm gone long
but no, you aren't really

you're sitting up someplace asleep
your head bobbing back until it almost
hits the wall behind you but then
you wake yourself up
either from the snoring
or from the faraway thought
it's time to get back on that bird and
fly south far into the greenest green
there is a jungle wide and jade
the beds there are hammocks

tied up to giant trees
en el Amazona
or closer to it than here
where air is lighter
but I want to breathe
the jade air with you
holding me in those arms so sure
I miss you seeing me

the real me I say doesn't exist
she ran and joined the circus and
I hate clowns
they are really masked killers
or close to it
mad or wicked or worse
you know the kind
that smile in your face
while twisting the knife that is not
sharp enough to kill quickly

I don't want a slow death
those don't run in my tree
the family likes to make
its mind up and just do it
go or die whatever comes first
water or guns
a few have chosen guns
but most have gone water
or with pills in their sleep
but then some woke up and
had bad nightmares of dying
with no say in the matter

where are you sleeping now
what chair in what airport
cradles your hunched body
will you miss that next plane
scheduled to fly over
the Patagonia

I send you a green kiss
wear it like a shamrock
for luck or love
or for safe journeying back home
to me in my hammock

The Energies ~ Orunmila and Tlaloc

Orunmila is the spirit of the wisdom to overcome life's misfortunes and the map to our destiny. Like the other Irunmole, entities sent by Olorun to complete given tasks, often acting as liaisons between Orun (the invisible realm) and Aiye (the physical realm) Orunmila existed before man and is said to have witnessed creation. He therefore has knowledge concerning the fate of all on the earth. He is the youngest of all the divine energies created by Olorun before the creation of the earth. He was incarnated, as were many of the Orisha, and sent to earth on various occasions, especially at times of great chaos, to assist mankind.

Orunmila is especially entrusted with helping people who have major life decisions to consider. Decisions which can have grave consequences on personal destiny. These are the great junctures of human life, and Esu-Elegua, who is charged with opening and closing the doors on the path of fulfilling our destinies, is the one who sits at this crossroads to serve and assist Orunmila and humankind as no other Orisha.

Ifa priests known as Babalawos represent Orunmila, they use the spirit's divinatory system, the sacred Ifa Oracle, and it's liturgical corpus, to guide people on how to conduct their lives. Through sacrifice and the development of good character humans are given the best formula for living a satisfying life.

Orunmila's colors are yellow and green or green and maroon. Some of his offerings include bread with epo - red palm oil, yams, red snapper, and white wine.

Tlaloc, He Who Makes Things Sprout [Grow], is the divinity of rain, of vegetation, and the ruler of the sacred south direction, known to the Olmec as *Epcoatl*, which means Sea Shell Serpent. The divinity of rain, known to the Maya as *Chac*, to the Totonacs as *Tajin*, to the Mixtecas as *Tzahui*, and to the Zapotecs as *Cocijo*. Lord of all sources of water, clouds, rains, lightning, and weather.

Tlaloc, is a greatly revered energy because it is believed that he is who sends rain to the people or can withhold it and thereby cause droughts, hunger and death. He is legend to have hurled lightning upon the earth and unleashed devastating windstorms in the form of hurricanes. The Tlaloque, Tlaloc's stewards who reside in the mountains, where rain and clouds are formed, are believed to be able to send down different types of rain, which are either helpful to, or destroy, the crops.

Tlaloc, the eighth ruler of the days and the ninth lord of the nights. Five months of the 18-month ritual year are dedicated to him and his attendants, the Tlaloque. Those who die from drowning, lightning strikes, or things thought to be associated with water go to Tlacocan, the paradise of Tlaloc located in the South, which is known as the place of fertility.

Tlaloc is easily identified by his characteristic mask, which gives the impression that he is wearing eyeglasses and has a moustache. Blue is the dominant color of his mask, and the color most associated with the divinity of rain though his body and face are often shown painted black.

With much respect for Orunmila and his children who are the interpreters of Odu, liturgical Yoruba, or Ifa; and to the mysteries of Tlaloc, the energy or manifestation of nature which embodies that sacred primary element.
Water is life.

Rainmaking

they prayed.
storms would not come.
he piled the hardwood high,
sat center, with flame-tongues rising
rains fell

full moon
wears an aura,
children sing the frog songs.
we pray along, with offerings
clouds burst

Science
the thinking man's
God, rules mother nature.
they seed clouds with silver dry ice…
deluge

warm clouds
super-cooled. fooled
fat formations circle
hit like a cold spoon, in sky-space
crying

sun baked
souls, smoke signal
desert ancestor winds.
rain shadows slowly sip the sky
water

to call
rain venerate
Chac. to implore the rain
venerate Tlaloc. to implore
the rain
dance   dance   dance

Ofrendas

a rock atop a headstone
marks my visit

rattlesnake tail earring
telegraphs a message in my right ear

red parrot tail feather
keeps my head straight

tears stream
ribbons of joy down my face

a glass full of river water
keeps away the tide of fear

white earth line drawn on center
keeps my head from being parted

black earth sprinkled in a yellow gourd
remembrance dust of my red ancestors

tears run uncontrollably south
stinging eyes cooled by release

lapis blue mussel shell washed up on the beach
sea foam reaches land grabs gently for my feet

sacrificial blood spilled in prayers
monthly lives are not conceived

white doves released in a black forest
a ring of trees rings another ring of trees

Poem 30 ~ Earth First

relics.
long buried frogs,
distinct in their knowledge
most coveted for their secrets,
of rain

precious
life's most sacred
liquid. world's creatures cry
for fortune, and nature to keep
giving

sunken
sounds spiraling,
as throngs in the heat, chant
for wet moon monsoons to explode
~ oceans

earth swells
with the icy
melt of blue-green glaciers
molting into frightening winter's ~
demons

unleashed
anew, as then,
when ancestors vanished
from old sicknesses, created ~
havoc

earth is
part suffering.
what survives – is coded.
steeped in DNA, in knowledge
of change

Teocintli

little sister
little brother
kernels of truth

tell me
tell me
what's become
of my youth

toss you once
toss you twice
we listen
to your sage
advice

seeds from the stars
golden flesh beads
god's sustenance
for the people

your heart worn
on the outside
knowledge and
nourishment

sacred mouths
we feed upon
your wisdom seeds

The Color of Light

is shadow
there is not one
without the other

to delve further
into this duality
one must vision

reality bent
a descent
into seeing

what isn't
a three-dimensional trick
in that world of flat magic

tragic when people refuse
to muse beyond
their edges

isn't it?
and color only
inside their lines

their whole lives spent
not looking beyond
their assigned comfort

not feeling the others
who live with us daily
sharing the planet

on an invisible level
or is it?
some same plane traffic jam

where some of us
are merely sideswiped while
others are rammed head-on

since birth in a collision
of unimaginable proportions
jolting us into the outer limits

of an extra sensory dispensary
never being able
to be quite right

in the eyes of those
who merely live
the blue light specials

and only consume life
through bright and shiny things
not on the margins

seeing the bigger picture
sacrificing
much more

than what is bargained for
but that would require
sight

beyond being stuck
with the silver spoon
while the sun

spins us wildly
forward
in its hoop

In the Line of Time

futures and pasts stop

dead in their tracks

forward   or rewind

not an option

here heaven dreams

are circles

portals to 25 years past

or was it a second ago

eating Thanksgiving

turkey in the raw

new-age adventurers

in a plum colored kitchen

a transport or a view

to a possible tomorrow

La Vista

left hand hides pebble
right hand bone
a voice in the querent's head
calls out switch hands
before it's too late
but bone jiggles toothily
in her hand and says
you can't change fate

pebble replies
that is why she's come
to hear the truth
of what's around the next turn
so she might swerve
or take less or no hit

just coming here
to face the sixteen mouths
open or shut
will pre-say
what is to come
as time moves on

she wonders
what in the *before*
led her to this place
that makes her so sad
hurt or want to run away

her hands stay closed
ibo firmly held
one on each leg
she feels as though
she's treading deep water
waiting for a life-saver a raft
but what comes is the sound

of the divining chain
being thrown down
an Odu
a sign
skittering across
yellow reed mat
the seer counts mouths

then motions *right hand*
within her left
a shadow of doubt
but here
one must not
wonder
what might
have been
we all have free will
to take the Oracles advice
or live the consequences

Poem 3 ~ Destiny

embracing your destiny
should be painless
as morning being birthed
through the aperture
of consecutive indigo
nights that pass through
the sieve of sky and amber stars
 rolling on low boil
it is not a TV drama
or the nightly done rightly news
though it may be stranger
than any writ down fiction
because most modern-day
humans act so hastily
yes, so often times stupidly
thinking tomorrows
won't catch up to them
in an eye-blink and disaster
has struck
people wail and weep
but keep on doing
the same unquestioning things
over and over again
just like our sunrise blooms
into another day
we expect to live just fine
but a nation can't sleep
knowing that Japan
is going down and no one
in power ever said let's stop
this obvious threat
when there was still a chance
daily billions are spent
on war and more people
are dying from this tech-no-
logic insanity
can't we help fix this now

in California we swim
the same sea
that washes up
thousands of miles
away
from the radiated
shores
just off
of Fukushima
and our nuclear power plants
San Onofre and Diablo Canyon
– the Saint and Devil twins –
sit waiting
on the fault line
for a destruction sure and
all we hear is the same
tongue wagging
the same lies
of yesteryear
it will never happen here …

A Blessing of Blue Corn

she plucks twelve kernels

of purple-blue corn from its ear

to have a future divined for her

she is nervous about the past

anxious for a future cast

yet, she is trying to decide

her path which seems to crash

down around her

whenever she thinks

she knows all the answers

from each direction

she asks for guidance

then enters inside and opens herself up

thirsting for possibilities

wondering what will be

foretold in which direction

she will ultimately   have to go

Oracle

the code

a codex with roads

right and detours

journeys   wild

with windstorms

leveling initiations

humbling gyrations

tumbling in ancients'

knowledge

that brings power

or a kind of madness

About The Author

Odilia Galván Rodríguez, poet, writer, editor, educator, and activist is the author of six volumes of poetry, her latest, The Nature of Things, a collaboration with Texas photographer, Richard Loya, by Merced College Press, 2016. Also, along with the late Francisco X. Alarcón, she edited the award- winning anthology: Poetry of Resistance: Voices for Social Justice, University of Arizona Press, 2016. This poetry of witness anthology, the first of its kind because it came about because of the primarily on-line organizing work of Alarcón, Galván Rodriguez, and other poet-activists which began as a response to the proposal of SB 1070, the racial profiling law which was eventually passed by the Arizona State Legislature in 2010 and later that year, HB 2281which banned ethnic studies. With the advent of the Facebook page Poets Responding (to SB 1070) thousands of poems were submitted witnessing racism, xenophobia, and other social justice issues which culminated in the anthology.

Galván Rodríguez has worked as an editor for various print media such as Matrix Women's News Magazine, Community Mural's Magazine, and Tricontinental Magazine in Havana, Cuba. She is currently, the director of Red Earth Productions and Cultural Work, publisher of Prickly Pear Publishing & Nopalli Press, the editor of Cloud Women's Quarterly Journal on line, and facilitates creative writing workshops nationally. She also manages Poets Responding, and Love and Prayers for Fukushima and the World, both Facebook pages dedicated to bringing attention to social justice issues that affect the lives and wellbeing of many people and encourages people to act. Her poetry has appeared in numerous anthologies, and literary journals on and off line.

As an activist she's worked for the United Farm Workers of America AFL-CIO, The East Bay Institute for Urban Arts, has served on numerous boards and commissions, and is currently active in Women's organizations whose mission it is to educate around women's rights, environmental justice issues and disseminate an Indigenous world view regarding the earth and people's custodial relationship to it. Odilia Galván Rodríguez has a long and rich history of working for social justice in solidarity with activists from all ethnic groups.

Bibliography and Sources

Abimbola, Wande. *Ifá Will Mend Our Broken World*. Aim Books, 1997.
Aguilar-Moreno, Manuel. *Handbook to Life in the Aztec World*. Oxford University Press, 2007.
Almere Read, Kay. Time and Sacrifice in the Aztec Cosmos. Bloomington/IN: Indiana Univ. Press 1998.
Bascom, William. *Sixteen Cowries Yoruba Divination from Africa to the New World*. Indiana University Press; Reprint edition, 1980.
Bierhorst, John. *Cantares Mexicanos: Songs of the Aztecs*. Translated from Nahuatl with an Introduction and Commentary by John Bierhorst. Stanford, CA: Sanford University Press, 1985.
_____. *History and Mythology of the Aztecs: The Codex Chimalpopoca*. University of Arizona Press, 1998.
_____. "On the Nature of Aztec Poetry," Review 29: 69—71. New York: Inter-American Relations, 1981.
_____. *The Sacred Path: Spells, Prayers and Power Songs of the American Indian*. New York: Quille, 1983.
Cabrera, Luis. *Diccionario de aztequismos*. Mexico City: Oasis, 1980.
Cardenal, Ernesto. *Quetzalcoatl*. Translated by Clifton Ross. Berkeley, CA: New Earth Publications, 1990.
Carrasco, Davíd. *Quetzalcóatl and the Irony of Empire*. Chicago: University of Chicago Press, 1982.
_____. (ed.) *The Imagination of Matter. Religion and Ecology in Mesoamerican Traditions*. Oxford: BAR Int'l Series 1989.
_____. (ed.) Lindsay Jones, Scott Sessions. Mesoamerica's Classic Heritage: Teotihuacan to the Aztecs. The University Press of Colorado, 2000.
Cartwright Brundage, Burr. *A Rain of Darts: The Mexica Aztecs*. University of Texas Press, 2014.
Clendinen, Inga. *Aztecs: An Interpretation*. Cambridge University Press, 1995.
de Sahagún, Fray Bernardino. *Florentine Codex. 14 volumes, second printing, transl. from the Nahuatl and Spanish by Arthur J. O. Anderson & Charles E. Dibble*. Santa Fe/NM: School of American Research, 1978.
Diaz, Gisele, Alan Rodgers. *The Codex Borgia: A Full-Color Restoration of the Ancient Mexican Manuscript*. Cambridge University Press, 1993.
Diaz del Castillo, J.M Cohen. *The Conquest of New Spain*. Penguin Books,1963.
Dice Ifa.
Epega, Aflolabi A. The Sacred Ifa Oracle (English and Yoruba Edition) HarperCollins 1st edition, 1995.
Fama, Chief. *Fundamentals of the Yoruba Religion (Orisa Worship)*. ILÉ Òrúnmìlà Communications; Revised 2nd edition, 2002.

Karade, Oloye. *The Handbook of Yoruba Religious Concepts.* Weiser Books. 1994.
Karttunen, Frances. *An Analytical Dictionary of Nahuatl.* Austin: University of Texas Press, 1983.
Leon-Portilla, Miguel. *Broken Spears: The Aztec Account of the Conquest of Mexico.* Beacon Press, Boston; First Edition, 1962.
_____. Jack Emory Davis. *Aztec Thought and Culture: A Study of the Ancient Nahuatl Mind.* University of Oklahoma Press; Revised ed. edition, 2012.
Miller, Mary and Karl Taube. *An Illustrated Dictionary of The Gods and Symbols of Ancient Mexico and the Maya.* Thames and Hudson, 1993,1997.
Phillips, Charles. *The Illustrated Encyclopedia of Aztec & Maya: The Greatest Civilizations of Ancient Central America with 1000 Photographs, Paintings & Maps.* Hermes House, 2017.
Séjourné, Laurette. *Burning Water: Thought and Religion in Ancient Mexico.* London: Thames and Hudson, 1957.
Soustelle, Jacques. *Daily Life of the Aztecs.* Stanford/CA: Stanford Univ. Press 1970

www.ingramcontent.com/pod-product-compliance
Lightning Source LLC
Chambersburg PA
CBHW080543090426
42734CB00016B/3187